NIGH ON SIXTY YEARS AT SEA

Yours faithfully
Robt J Woodward

NIGH ON SIXTY
YEARS AT SEA

BY

ROBERT WOOLWARD

'OLD WOOLWARD'

WITH PORTRAIT

LONDON

DIGBY, LONG & CO., PUBLISHERS

18 BOUVERIE STREET, FLEET STREET, E.C.

PREFACE.

———

FOR some years I have contemplated writing an account of my voyages, but leisure
for this has been wanting. This is due
to the fact that I have constantly been
making runs to and from the West Indies.
In March 1893, however, I was compelled
to remain at home, and very soon after
the ship had sailed without me I found
myself at some loss as to what use to
make of my time. The ladies of my
household occasionally reminded me that
an idle man about the house, especially
in the early part of the day, is not quite
welcome to them. I, therefore, turned my

attention to the preparation of a record of my experiences during nigh thrice a score of years, and these experiences are here recorded for the benefit of the reader.

Will my work succeed? Well, one of our great writers has assured me that my chronicle is too truthful, and that the public rather leans to aspiring fiction, not to use a harsher word, in these matters. Sailors are a truthful folk, however, and I have only set down the things that really occurred. What these things are the reader will discover for himself, and I can promise that, besides being strange, these things are true.

CONTENTS.

PART I.

PART II.

b

CONTENTS.

PART I.

Nigh on Sixty Years at Sea

CHAPTER I.

I DON'T suppose it matters a brass farthing to anyone when or where I was born, but as this is meant to be my history, the first thing about it is that I must, of necessity, have been born somewhere.

This interesting event took place in the Pier House at Ramsgate, and if ever a poor woman found herself possessed with a bundle of mischief, that woman was my dear mother, on the morning of April 15th, 1826.

The first trouble was that all the boat-repairing business, usually carried on at a place called The Lockers (I can't say if that is the right way of spelling it), just in front of the house, had to be stopped, and this caused a good deal of bickering between the boatmen

A

and the two pier policemen, 'Paddy Ryan' and 'Sergeant Manning,' who, being old soldiers, would give no other explanation than 'it is the harbour-master's orders.' Now, the harbour-master was my father, and, being one of the old-fashioned Royal Naval officers, he did not allow any questioning of his orders, so there was no use for anyone to appeal, and the folks had simply to grin and bear it, and content themselves, as they usually did, by swearing at the author of their trouble, and take the boat somewhere else to repair—rather a troublesome job, perhaps, as, by the time they were stopped, a plank would have been taken out of the boat, and it would not float.

Matters went on pretty smoothly, as far as I have been given to understand, till I was old enough to run about the pier-yard, and then my mischievous propensities began to develop themselves.

At that period Ramsgate had not got over the Buonaparte scare. The pier was armed with 32-pounder guns, and the shot was piled up in various places. My great delight was to roll them off the pile, when no one was looking, to the great danger of my fingers and toes, and the disgust of Jemmy Wait, the old sweeper, who had to put them up again. This mischief was soon traced to me, and Paddy Ryan kept watch, with the result that I was caught and, according to his orders, got locked up in the pier-cage, and kept there till after dinner-time. When I got home the reason of my absence was apparently only known by the coal-tar on my hands. Of course, for the future I did not meddle with the shot, but other boys did, and I got the full credit of it till another boy was caught; but then I was in trouble, as the boy's mother said I put him up to do it, which was fully believed.

I am afraid, as I grew older, I did not improve, and, when I was sent to the Dame's school, I became acquainted with a boy of my own age, called Billy Green, and we were, forthwith, sworn allies.

I was generally sent to school and fetched by a girl called Hannah Nicholls, the daughter of one of the pier-men. This was all very well for a time, whilst I had a little fear of the school 'Marm' (as our American cousins would call the good lady); but my friend Billy Green, who went to and fro by himself, began to taunt me with being in charge of a girl, so one fine day Hannah arrived home without me, holding her apron up to her nose, which was bleeding from the effects of a missile, in the shape of a sheep's foot, which I had thrown at her. This mutinous conduct, as my father termed it, had to be put a stop to, and I was punished in the way that was more fashionable in those days than now. I may say I did not feel comfortable sitting on the form at school for some days after, so my young friends in misfortune may be able to guess what shape the punishment took.

I soon got too 'owdacious' for the Dame's school, and, at the age of nine, was handed over to Thomas Whitehead, Esq. (commonly called Old Tim by the boys), of Chatham House Academy, and, for the future, there was no need to punish me at home, as Old Tim was fully equal to the job, and, when necessary, I was made the bearer of a small note which always had the postage levied on it on delivery.

There is no doubt in my mind, now, that Mr Whitehead was an excellent preceptor. He knew the character of every boy in the school—(there were always ninety-nine boarders; he would not have one hundred), and, no matter what mischief was reported to him, he decided at once which boy did it, and, after prayers in the morning, it was, 'Boy so-and-so step this way,' and he said to him, 'Now, sir, why did you do—?' whatever it might be. He never asked *whether* you did it;

he felt certain about it, and I never knew him to be in error.

And the school was in other respects a good one.

There was plenty of wholesome food and plenty of hard work. I and the other day - boys had to be at school at 5.40 A.M., and we were not allowed to go home till 8.20 P.M., after prayers. This sort of training very few boys of the present day could stand, but I never knew of any of them breaking down. It is true that no weakly boy was received; Mr Whitehead saying that Chatham House was not an hospital. I suppose it was necessary, on account of the short time— most boys leaving school at fourteen, and being bound apprentices to whatever business they were to follow.

Thus, on 29th April, 1840, I had left school and was apprenticed to one Mr Gunstan of London, the owner, among other vessels, of the brig 'Diadem' (called 'Didaddem' by the sailors), engaged in the timber - trade. We sailed for Quebec on 29th April, and I found that school, hard as I thought it, was quite a pleasure compared to the routine in the brig. Watch and watch was hard enough, but it was always all hands in the afternoon.

The crew of the brig consisted of ten, all told. The master and mate had been apprentices to the same owner, as also had William, the second mate, but, after William had served his time at sea, he was apprenticed to the shipbuilder at Sunderland who built Mr Gunstan's vessels, and so was qualified as second mate and carpenter; with the exception of an old sailor, David Rees by name, the rest were apprentices, and generally under the charge of old David, who repaired the sails and instructed us generally in rigging work.

As I was the youngest apprentice, I had to be cook and steward, and did not keep any watch; as soon as I could be instructed, I had to take the helm from four till six in the morning watch, and from six till eight in the evening. It was not many days before I was able to steer as well as any of them, having learnt to steer the boats at Ramsgate, and to box the compass at school, but old David took the credit of it, begging me not to tell the master, who was quite at a loss to understand how a green-hand, and a gentleman's son, could so soon have learnt to do what it generally took others at least a whole voyage to pick up. As long as the brig was sailing on a wind, I could manage perfectly; but, going large, my strength was not always equal to the work, the brig being steered with a tiller.

The principal work on the passage was the

repairing an old ship gig, which the master had bought cheap and intended to sell for a good price. It was quite astonishing how that boat got renovated under the hands of William and the master, who was a very fair boat-builder, his father having been in that line; and when it was put in the water, on arrival at Quebec, it looked quite like a new one, and was sold to one of the rowing clubs for £20. We saw it win a prize at the regatta before we sailed for home.

We had generally fine weather on the way out, but had a narrow escape of getting wrecked on Cape Race in a gale of wind, which made it a lee-shore; the brig being in ballast was barely able to claw off, and must have gone ashore had not the wind shifted suddenly in the middle watch.

A few days after this we got into the River St Lawrence, and had to anchor every time it was high water, as the wind blew right down the river. One night we anchored off some islets called the Brandy-pots, and I was left on watch with old Rees. A boat came off from the shore, and as there was no tobacco on board, very little having been brought away in the vessel, old Rees wanted to get some from the boatmen; of course, he had no money, and tobacco was not to be got for nothing, so some of the vessel's stores had to be given in exchange. We had made, on the passage, two long gaskets for the boom main-sail; one of these the boatmen wanted, to make their sail fast, so old David sent me up to take it off, and he swapped it for two plugs of Cavendish.

I was so disgusted at this that I there and then made a resolution, to which I have always adhered, that I would never use tobacco. Fortunately the gasket was not missed, as old David very soon made another.

On a Sunday morning in May, we arrived at Quebec and anchored in the ballast ground; the approach was very beautiful after having seen nothing but water and rugged shores for a month. I was particularly struck with the sun shining on the zinc-covered roofs of the houses, and the hundreds of vessels at anchor.

As we dropped towards the anchorage, we were nearly in collision with a huge raft of timber, and a good deal of very bad French was exchanged between our pilot and the inhabitants of the raft, which was at anchor near to Point Tear, waiting the turn of the tide; fortunately a puff of wind came and we were able to make a stern board and cleared it.

Now began the heaviest work of the voyage, viz., heaving the ballast overboard—this we had to do ourselves, as the master would not employ labour and we were not used to shovelling. I had to stand with the next older apprentice on a stage slung up a little below the ballast port; the others hove the sand up on to the stage and we had to shovel it out; fortunately my mate was a strong, good-natured lad, and did far more than his share of the work. It is astonishing how much more attention than usual that galley-fire required, whilst the ballast business was going on!

However, all things come to an end, and by the Saturday night the ballast was out and we had Sunday to move the vessel over to Diamond Harbour, where we were to load. We got her moored by dinner-time, and were allowed to go ashore afterwards.

I made at once for Wolfe's Monument, and thought I was never going to get there, as, not having done any walking for six weeks, my feet and legs were not quite fit for such a climb; possibly I did not arrive in a very good humour, but I decided it was a very mean monument to make so much talk about, and that it was not to be compared to *our* obelisk at Ramsgate.

After resting some time I started back again, and in due time arrived down abreast the brig, and made my first acquaintance with a sailor's public-house, called the 'Strop and Block,' with an invitation to sailors in the following verse:—

> Brother sailor, pray thee stop
> And lend me a hand to strop this block,
> For if you do not stop with speed,
> I cannot strop this block indeed.

Such a pressing invitation, of course, could not be refused, so I went in and found plenty of sailors, not stropping blocks indeed, but in various stages of drunkenness. These men had mostly deserted from ships, which at that time was the fashion. A few nights after the ship arrived, there would be a general clear-out of the crew, who then got shipped in a loaded vessel, at a very high rate for the run. They did not lose anything by deserting, or very little, as they had received a month's advance before leaving England; neither did they make much by the high-rate homeward, as the landlords of such places as the 'Strop and Block' kept them whilst in Quebec, and, of course, charged a very high price for the accommodation and keeping them drunk all the time he had them on his hands.

Thus I discovered the wisdom of our owner in having his vessels manned, or rather, perhaps, 'boyed' (if I may be allowed to coin a word) by apprentices. I was not allowed to remain in this house. The landlady gave me some milk and a biscuit and told me 'to clear out;' she did not 'allow brats about her premises, spying and then informing the masters where to find their men.

She did not charge me anything for what I had, so I concluded she took the value out in abuse, and I was quite satisfied to let it be so, as the good woman kept her hands off.

As the brig was chartered to take timber for the Woolwich Dockyard, it did not require very long to get loaded, and on the Sunday fortnight we were under weigh for home.

We had a fair wind all the way from the Island of St Paul's till we arrived off the North Foreland, thence a dead beat up to Woolwich.

On arrival there we found something had gone wrong with the owner, and, after discharging, the vessel, was put up for sale and all of us sent home for the time being.

CHAPTER II.

IN the spring of 1841, by the interest of my god-father, Captain Robert Welbank, one of the Elder Brethren of the Trinity House, my indentures were transferred to Mr Joseph Soames, and I was sent on board a vessel called 'La Belle Alliance,' fitting out as an armed transport to join the China Expedition. She was loading Government stores off the victualling yard at Deptford.

This was quite a different line to the one in which I had made a start. Instead of a small crew consisting of a few apprentices, this vessel, although only 676 tons registered, carried a crew with a boatswain who piped, as also his two mates, forty A.B.'s, twenty O.S., eight landsmen and seven apprentices. The crew were brought alongside and shipped on board (there not being any shipping offices in those days). They were supplied by a crimp whom the sailors called Ned Skeet, and with whom a good many had been boarding.

Having signed the articles and received two months' advance (or rather, when notes for the same had been handed to Mr Skeet), several gentlemen of the Hebrew persuasion came up the side and opened slop-shops about the deck, as Mr Skeet was too prudent to allow any of his mob out of the ship, and the men had to make up their outfit for the voyage. For such things as they bought Mr Skeet paid cash, of course taking care that the purchases each man made left a good margin in his hands to pay for any board that might be owing to him.

It may thus be inferred that Jack's outfit was not a very splendid one, and he had soon to draw on the ship's slop-chest.

Towards 3 P.M. the same day, everyone but the crew and Mr Skeet's two auxiliaries were ordered out of the ship, which was unmoored and taken in tow as far as Gravesend, where we anchored for the night.

Towards noon the next day a Government tug brought down some officials, who inspected the ship, numbered the crew, and then handed the vessel over to the charge of Lieutenant Densten, R.N., who received his appointment from them, as agent of H.M. Hired Transport, No. 15. The red ensign we had been flying was hauled down, and a blue ensign, with a large yellow anchor in the fly of it, hoisted; also a blue pennant, with a yellow anchor in it, was hoisted at the main.

We received from the tug a four-oared gig, and a cabin table for the agent's use, and the ship was declared in all respects ready for sea.

This ceremony being ended, and all strangers being out of the ship, we weighed, and were towed down to Pausand Hole, where we again anchored for the night. Having now been left to our own devices, and the wind being foul, we remained at anchor all the next day. The crew were divided into watches, and the station-bill made out. The men were also told off to the guns, of which there were ten 24-pounder carronades.

At daylight the next morning we were under weigh, and got down to the Downs, where the pilot left, and the ship went on, till, in a day or two, we anchored in Plymouth Sound. I have forgotten to mention that there were eight assistant-surgeons on board, going to join the fleet in China. These gentlemen each occupied a cabin under the poop, and were the only passengers we had leaving London.

On arrival at Plymouth, orders were received to land a portion of the stores we had taken in at Deptford, to make room for the construction of a magazine on the lower deck beams, from the main to the fore-hatch, as we were to take out live-shell.

This being done, several dockyard officials came on board, looked at the space, and went away again. Two days after, a lighter came alongside with planks, which were taken on deck. The next day some shipwrights came off and brought their tools, but as the foreman did not come, nothing could be done, and, one way and another, it was quite a week before the magazine was commenced, and it took a fortnight before it was completed, inspected, and pronounced fit to receive the shell, etc.

In the course of another week it got filled, and it was then found the ship was required to carry out a suit of sails for each ship on the station, and the question arose how this could be done. However, the agent suggested to the admiral taking half the cabins occupied by the assistant-surgeons for the sails. This measure was adopted, and without further loss of time the sails were stowed away and the ship sailed.

At Plymouth we also took on board one hundred marines and forty boys, for service with the fleet; altogether, the ship was well filled!

Nothing eventful happened on the passage. We called at Teneriffe and replenished the live stock and fresh water, and arrived at Simson

Bay (Cape of Good Hope) in due course, having lost both topgallant masts whilst beating in.

The passage was enlivened by the constant quarrels that took place between the agent and the assistant-surgeons, who did not forgive him for getting them put two in a cabin. Whilst in Simon's Bay we landed all the sails and opened them out to air in the dockyard; this, of course, took some time, as also did filling in the fresh water. I had noticed on the way out that there did not appear any hurry about anything. The ship was put under easy sail every night before dark, and royal-yards sent down, the agent not allowing too much sail to be carried. The least puff of wind brought the old gentleman out of his cabin, and he called out to the captain,—

'Mr Pryce, Mr Pryce, I won't have Her Majesty's stores endangered!'

I wondered why his orders were so promptly carried out, till I found the ship was paid by the month, and it was, of course, to the owner's interest to be as long as possible on the passage, besides saving the wear and tear in carrying too much sail.

In due time we sailed again, with orders not to call in anywhere till we reached Hong-Kong. This was a work of time, as, by one delay and another, we had lost the season and the N.E. monsoon had commenced in the China Sea. We got short of water and fresh provisions, and were generally uncomfortable on board, notwithstanding we had disobeyed orders and called off Angeir, going through the Strait of Java.

The crew did not consider fowls were fresh provisions, and would have nothing to do with them except they were pickled, so they had to go on with the salt-provisions and have lime juice served out to them. This lime juice had to be drawn from the Government stores, as merchant ships did not carry it in those days. Altogether, we were very glad to arrive, which we did after having been six months and twenty-one days from Plymouth.

We found Hong-Kong had been taken, and the fleet, except H.M.S. 'Herald' and 'Alligator' had sailed for the north, so, after having recruited a bit and filled up the fresh water, we sailed to join the fleet at Amoy on 23rd November, 1841. The ship, being deeply laden, made bad work of beating up against the monsoon, and after being fourteen days out, we sighted Formosa, where, a gale of wind coming on, we stood across and came to an anchor at the island of Leuconia, having lost jib-boom and head-gear and carried away the main top-sail yard.

Whilst lying there matters between the agent and the assistant-surgeons grew serious. The agent had complained against them to Captain Ryas of the 'Herald,' who was the senior naval officer; an inquiry was held, and it was decided there were faults on both sides.

A sort of a truce was patched up, but the agent would not mess at the cuddy table, and the truce was broken as soon as we got to sea again, with the result that, now we were at anchor, in a place without any authority to prevent it, a duel was resolved on.

Accordingly, one morning the agent landed in his gig, of which I was the coxswain, and the captain and two of the surgeons landed in the Captain's gig. The agent fought each of the surgeons. The agent got shot through his stern parts from right to left, and shot his first antagonist in the left arm. In what may be called the second round, the agent went clear, but he put a shot through his opponent's neck, fortunately without touching any vital part. However, all three parties were disabled; the remaining surgeons were occupied in attending to the wounded, and hostilities were suspended.

By this time the ship had been refitted, and we started again for Amoy, but only succeeded in making the S.E. end of Formosa, and then bore away for Hong-Kong, where we arrived the day before Christmas, considerably the worse for the weather.

Here we found H.M.S. 'Blenheim' and 'Nimrod,' in addition to the 'Herald' and 'Alligator;' the latter was about to sail to join the fleet, so the surgeons, marines and boys were turned over to her. We were relieved of a good deal of heavy stores, and generally refitted. H.M.S. 'Sulphur' also arrived, and the shell we had on board being for her, we handed it over, and by the help of working parties from the 'Blenheim' we were soon ready for sea again, and sailed under orders to proceed to Chusan, as Amoy had been left under a small garrison.

The captain of the 'Blenheim' also impressed on the agent that he was not to interfere with the sailing of the ship, as most likely the master would know more about it than he did. So, having got rid of the pugnacious doctors, and the ship being clear of the marines and boys, we had more room to work, and were at peace.

We took the eastern passage and arrived at Chusan in about three weeks, where we found the whole of the expedition, consisting of H.M.S. fleet, under Admiral Sir Wm. Parker in the 'Cornwallis,' and about a hundred sail of transports, making preparations for the next campaign.

Our ship was placed in the second division, and we were watered, filled up with wood, etc., in due course, and otherwise made ready to receive three companies of the 18th Royal Irish Regiment.

We were no longer allowed to go along in the same slow way we had pursued on the passage out. The officer in command of the division visited each ship belonging to it daily, and the agent had to send in a daily report of what work had been done. All this work was carried on very systematically. The boats of all the ships in the division were employed carrying water, wood, and stores for one or perhaps two ships in the same division, till they were filled up. On board these ships were working parties from the man-of-war in command of the division, and in charge of an officer. The crews of the ships had to stow the hold whilst the R.N. folks hoisted in. This plan accustomed the crews of the transports to working in the boats, and ensured the boats being kept in efficient working order. All this was particularly necessary, as the success of the expedition depended considerably on good boating services, and there were fire-rafts as well.

Everything was ready at last, and all the admiral's fleet assembled by the middle of April, and we sailed for Foo-chow. Now began the interesting part of the work, viz., fleet-sailing. We were divided into five divisions and sailed in two lines.   H.M.S. 'Cornwallis' with the flag led the first division, having always one of the few steamers attached to the expedition on his star-board hand, and a small schooner called the 'Hebe' sailing a little in advance, sounding all the time.

H.M.S. 'Blonde' was the whipper-in of the fleet, and had a pretty onerous task, as she had to look after all the slow sailers, which were placed in the fifth division, and was not allowed to anchor at night till she had seen all the ships anchored in their proper station.

Many ships found it a very difficult job to keep their station, and were constantly having the signal displayed to them—'Make more sail.'   On one occasion a vessel called the 'Alibi,' which had every stitch of canvas set, and still lagged, had this signal made to her, and having no more sail to set, the captain hoisted his house flag and sent a boy out to his weather main-royal yardarm to hold the flag out.   On seeing this, the whole of the trans-ports in his division hoisted the signal, 'Well done, "Alibi,"' to the great disgust of the man-of-war who led the division, and it was not long before the signal was flying,—'"Alibi," send a boat on board,' which would give him a lot of trouble, as he would have to drop his dispatch sailing boat and get her alongside the man-of-war, when he could, which most likely would not be before the fleet came to an anchor for the night, except the breeze fell light.

The transports were all kept in crack order and discipline ; we were all under martial law, and had to manœuvre the same as men-of-war, and a slack ship always got a good drilling somehow or other.

There certainly was no excuse for slackness, as all the ships carried heavy crews, and most of them had soldiers on board, who did all the rope hauling. At the same time nothing in the world would make some of the lumbering craft keep their stations, and H.M.S. 'Blonde' had a high old time of it.

Foo-chow was taken and burnt, and the fleet sailed to rendezvous at the Rugged Islands, each division with orders to make its own way, and the fifth division was to weigh first, which it did with six hours' start of the fourth.

Each division had to wait six hours, and then weigh, so the fifth division had all of twenty-four hours' start of the first, and still was the last to arrive at the rendezvous.

Whilst at anchor at the Rugged Islands, the force of the expedition was considerably increased. The 98th Regiment arrived in H.M.S. 'Belle Isle' and two native regiments in transports. H.M.S. 'Driver' and East India Company's steamship 'Tenasserim' also joined, and H.M.S. 'Dido' came before we left for Woosung, situated at the mouth of the river Yang-tse-Kiang.

On arriving off that place, we found a long row of mud batteries mounted with long brass guns. This place had to be taken by the men-of-war before we could proceed.

Accordingly, on the Monday morning, all the ships of the Royal Navy weighed, and took up positions close in to the battery, the smaller vessels leading and proceeding towards the end further up the river.

The battery commenced firing at them, but no notice was taken till all the ships had anchored, when the signal was given to 'open fire,' and it was not very long before most of the battery guns were silenced.

The troops had been got into the transports' boats in the meantime, and were ordered to land, under cover of the guns of the men-of-war.

There was no trouble about it, as, by the time we got to the beach, all the Chinamen that had not been killed, bolted, and all was over by dinner-time—not a single man of the attacking force being hurt.

During the week we were employed in getting

the brass guns out of the battery on board the various transports. They were long and heavy, but could only fire in one direction, as they were all fixed on the carriages, which were fixed in the ground.

We also had a good deal of work to bury the dead Chinamen, all of whom had been left when the skeedaddle took place.

Everything was ready for a move again by the end of the week, and on the Sunday a transport called the 'Teazer' arrived, bringing news of a Royal birth, and also the promotion of the admiral from Rear-Admiral of the Red to Vice-Admiral of the Blue, so all the men-of-war first fired a Royal salute on account of the birth of H.R.H. the Prince of Wales, and afterwards saluted the admiral's new flag.

This 'Teazer' was a chartered dispatch-vessel, and was certainly the smartest craft I have ever seen; barque-rigged, manned by Lascars, and sailed to perfection. Nothing in the fleet could touch her, either in sailing or exercise; she had been an opium clipper, and well designed that. This was the first news we had received from home since leaving Plymouth twelve months before.

On the Monday, early in the morning, we commenced getting ready to proceed up the river to capture Shanghai. The 'Hebe' had been busy during the week in taking soundings, and it was decided none of the ships were to go up ; it was to be entirely a boat service, with the exception of the three flat-bottomed steamers—the ' Nemesis,' ' Phlegethon ' and ' Pluto.'

These three vessels took on board as many men as they could accommodate standing on their decks, of the 18th Royal Irish, 26th Cameronians and the 55th Regiments, and the remainder were in boats taken in tow by the steamers, as also were the boats of the men-of-war, manned and armed.

We started at early dawn on the Tuesday morning, and arrived up at the city about nine o'clock.

The boats belonging to the men-of-war, of which there were at least fifty, including the flats (with one of which each ship was provided), commenced the attack, and as soon as the garrison were thrown into confusion, the troops were landed and took the guns in the rear (they were all fixed, the same as at Woosung). At the same time the marines landed in the face of the battery, and Mr China-man found himself nonplussed ; there was a pretty good slaughter, as both the troops and the marines ran on them with fixed bayonets, delivering a volley when they came to close quarters.

Our men suffered very little, but still we did not

get off as well as at Woosung; several men got killed, and others were wounded from the fire of the jinghals, a kind of a blunderbuss mounted on a short pedestal.

At the taking of Shanghai a good deal of plunder fell into the hands of the captors.

The main body of the attacking force were taken back to the ships that night, but a considerable number of the 55th Regiment were left quartered in the city, and part of the boat flotilla were left to guard the approach both above and below the city for the night.

They were relieved in the morning by the three steamers, and rejoined their ships.

The batteries were destroyed during the week, and the brass guns removed into one of the light draught transports which was sent up for them.

We next commenced the ascent of the mighty river Yang-tse-Kiang. From the anchorage off Woosung, the land at the opposite side could not be seen from the royal mast-head. We started with the whole fleet and the troops (Shanghai having been evacuated), and sailed in the same order, viz., five divisions and two lines, but as the wind was blowing up (the summer monsoon having set in) we had only to carry sail enough to keep station all day and anchor in deep water every night, till we arrived just below the Golden

Islands, near to which was the city of Ching-Kiang-Fu, and was the next place to be taken.

This city had a canal leading up to it and passing through, and presented considerable difficulty to the attack. However, the arrangements were soon made, but the men-of-war could not take any great part, except with their boats.

Only H.M.S. 'Driver' and the 'Tenasserim' were engaged, but they did great execution with shell and rockets at the lower part of the city.

The 'Driver' had command of a bridge leading from one of the islands to the city, and whilst the 'Tenasserim' shelled the island and drove the people out, the 'Driver' fired rockets along the bridge and we saw the Chinese sent flying over the parapet into the river. Here two ships were able to command the east gate of the city, so the 26th Regiment, who were told off for the attack of it, had good support and were very soon in possession.

All four gates were attacked simultaneously, but three of the assaulting parties only had the men-of-war's boats to cover the landing, and the force sustained great loss from the fire of the jinghals placed everywhere on the banks of the canal.

Whilst passing under one of the bridges, which had been cut away at both ends, it fell on two boats belonging to H.M.S. 'Blonde,' and as the crews were floundering in the mud and water, being under fire of the enemy on the bank, they lost one of the guns for a time, but other boats coming up it was recovered, and some troops effected a landing a little lower down. The banks were soon cleared and the rest of the troops landed, as also the artillery, and it was not very long before all four of the gates had been taken.

The day was intensely hot, and the men of the 98th Regiment suffered very much ; in fact, at night-fall, they could not even find a guard for the gate they had taken.

This was the first time they had been landed since embarking in England, and were sent on shore with all their equipments, shakos, and knap-sacks, whereas the men of the other regiments were only wearing shell-jackets and forage-caps with white covers, and instead of their packs, carried only their great-coats, with a blanket and spare shirt stowed inside.

We remained at anchor off Ching-Kiang-Fu for a fortnight, and were on shore and about the city a good deal.

This city had never been entered by foreigners before, and it offered a good deal for study, and there was plenty of what were termed

'curios' to be picked up (we did not buy anything).

We found what corresponded to pawn-shops at
home, filled with a very miscellaneous assortment
of goods. There were large quantities of winter
clothing, tied up in bundles, with small pieces of
bamboo for labels. So we came to the conclusion that, during the summer season, the good folks
pawned their winter-clothes. I am afraid, when
they were wanted, they would not be forthcoming,
as the barbarians carried them off.

The Chinese designated us barbarians, and I
have since thought we thoroughly deserved the
name. We appropriated, everywhere we went,
whatever took our fancies, and knocked the owners
down if they attempted to prevent their goods
being carried off.

This sort of behaviour was not according to the
ideas of the commanders of the expedition, and
the orders against it were very stringent, and I have
known several marauders taken red-handed by the
Provost-Marshal's people, seized up and given fifty
lashes there and then. I was never sufficiently unfortunate to get caught, neither were any of my
shipmates, but we deserved it as much as those
that were.

Captain Peter Richards, the flag-captain, was
particularly zealous in endeavouring to protect the

natives; he used to go about in the boats of the transports in mufti when he was on his thief-catching expeditions, and on one occasion, as he was on his way on shore in a boat belonging to No. 23, he met a boat of No. 167 going off loaded with sugar, taken from a large store near the north-gate.

As he passed, the captain of No. 167 hailed him and said,—

'You are too late, old fellow, I have got the last of the white, and by the time you get on shore all the brown will be gone.'

When Captain Richards went in a transport's boat, he always took his coxswain with him, so he said to No. 167,—

'Hold on a bit, I will come alongside and perhaps you will give me a sample?'

The man was green enough to do this, and as soon as the two boats came together, Captain Richards and his coxswain dropped into No. 167, and ordered them to pull alongside the flagship; but what happened when they got there we did not hear, as No. 167 did not belong to our division. We had at least a hundred bags of this sugar on board our ship, which were sold when we got down to Hong-Kong.

CHAPTER III.

WHEN we moved again with the fleet we went without our three companies of the Royal Irish, as that regiment was left to garrison Ching-Kiang-Fu, but we were turned into a hospital-ship and began to receive the sick of the 98th Regiment from the Belle Isle, on board which ship fever and dysentery had broken out amongst the troops.

We were quite full before we reached Nankin, at which place we arrived about a fortnight after. The progress was very slow, as we lost help from the tides, which were not felt after we got above the Golden Islands.

The current always ran down the river, and as we got higher up the wind got lighter. I have seen our vessels sailing with studding sails, set low and aloft and on both sides, for a whole day, and still keeping abreast the same tree on the bank, anchoring at night in exactly the same place as we had the previous night.

When we arrived at Nankin, we found flags of truce flying all over the walls of the city, so no attack was made, and after a few days we heard that a treaty of peace had been signed by the Chinese authorities and the Plenipotentiary, who was carried on board the 'Cornwallis.'

A large sum was to be paid for the expenses of the war, and sundry ports in the Celestial Empire were to be open for English commerce. Hong-Kong was also to be retained by the English.

The money was to be paid at once, so, in a few days, the boats of our division were employed in receiving bars of silver and taking them alongside the two men-of-war which were to carry them to England. Each of the boats so employed had two marines put into it to guard the treasure —we were not sure against whom, but concluded it was the boats' crews, as there was not the slightest chance of any Chinamen attempting to touch it.

Notwithstanding peace was proclaimed, we still had to be on the alert against junks, loaded with stones nearly to the water's edge, coming on us at night, the same as had been happening previously all the way up the river.

Whilst we were at Chusan, they sent down fire-rafts on us more than once; the last time was the

14th April, just before we left, but the guard boats gave us notice in good time, and we had our boats manned and kept them clear of the ship, by throwing grapplings on them and a towing chain attached to the boat. Each ship's boats had to keep ahead of its own ship, ready to take the raft in tow, in case there was any chance of its getting across the hawse.

Everything being settled up at Nankin, the transports were ordered to take in the troops left at Ching-Kiang-Fu, as they passed that city, and find their way down to Chusan.

We were to sail in company with the 'Belle Isle,' and to be under the orders of Captain Kingcombe, who commanded her.

We got down past the Golden Islands right enough, losing several of our sick soldiers every day, and those that were alive looked more like skeletons than anything else; so bad were they with dysentery that we made all the haste possible, keeping under way all night so as to reach Chusan and get the poor fellows landed.

The second day after passing the islands, the 'Belle Isle' got ashore on a sand-bank and, failing to back off, made us come to an anchor right astern of him, at one cable distance, he remaining under all sail, with everything aback.

We had not been long at anchor, and had

barely got our sails furled, when the 'Belle Isle' came off, and before he could fill, got across our hawse, carrying away our bowsprit, cut-water fore-royal-mast, topgallant-mast and topmast, making us a perfect wreck forward.

As soon as he got clear, he continued his way down, leaving us to shift for ourselves as we best could. Fortunately we had a large spar on board, with which we rigged a jury bowsprit and jib-boom, but as it was not equal to the strain of the forestays, they had to be set up to the knight heads and passed down under and abaft the fore-yard, and secured to the foremast with trappings.

This took away from us the use of the foresail, and we were obliged to back and fill all the way down the river under top-sails, topgallant-sails, jib and driver, instead of beating down as the other ships did. We also had to anchor as soon as the flood-tide made, having got hold of the tide again. This caused our progress to be very tedious, to say nothing of the hard work; several of our crew were getting intermittent fever, and we were obliged to keep our large sailing-boat in advance, sounding, as there were no charts to work by.

However, we got down all right as far as the entrance to Chusan Harbour, and we remained at anchor there till assistance was sent. H.M.S. 'Driver' came out and towed us in, but we had been so long getting down, that we had only eighteen soldiers to land out of the two hundred and eighty we took on board—all the rest we had buried on the way.

We remained at Chusan about three weeks, getting a new bowsprit made. We were able to get a large spar from the 'Sir Thomas Coutes,' a ship belonging to the same owner, and by building on it, brought it up to the size required. The only trouble we had was the want of iron hoops for it; this we tided over by using chain and iron wedges.

As soon as we were ready for sea, we were ordered to proceed to Hong-Kong, there to land all Government stores, and be paid off.

Of course, under these circumstances, it was not to be expected that we should try our bowsprit too much (anyhow we did not), and so made another long passage. We managed to spend another Christmas Day at Hong-Kong, and it was the end of January before we had finally left H.M. Service.

There was nothing in the way of freight to be got at Hong-Kong, so we went in ballast to Singapore, took in a part cargo there, and went on to Bombay.

We made another long passage and arrived there in sixty-seven days.

As the ship had been on shore more than once whilst in the transport service, we were obliged to go into dry-dock, get repaired and be surveyed before we could get a cargo. All the crew, therefore, were paid off, and we went in for a thorough overhaul.

This completed, we got a cargo of gum and cotton for Whampoa in China, and sailed for that place with the S.W. monsoon blowing, and arrived in thirty-two days.

We were very fortunate in getting a cargo at all, as so many transports had been discharged, and were all about seeking freights.

A few nights before we left Bombay, we saw the ship 'Sir Thomas Granville' burnt. It was a splendid sight, but one that made me feel very queer, as I pictured to myself what such a sight would mean at sea, and in the ship's boats and no one to look at it but ourselves.

Arrived at Whampoa, the work of unloading soon began, and it was very amusing to see the Chinaman, who was receiving the cargo, at his work.

He had a large pair of scales set up inside the gangway, and every bale of cotton was weighed. There were two kinds of bales; one he called 'Buffalo bale,' the other 'Pate bale' (Patent bale), and as each one passed the scale his man called out the mark and number and 'Buffalo bale, 3 cwt.,

3 qrs., 14 lbs.,' or 'Pate bale, 3 cwt., 0 qrs., 14 lbs.,' all in a language called Pigeon-English.

The bale then had a piece of bamboo stuck in it, which was taken out by the man in the chop, or lighter, alongside. When the lighter was loaded a boat note was given to the captain of the chop, who compared it with the number of sticks he had, and, if it tallied, he delivered up the sticks to the Chinaman on deck, ready to be used with the next chop; but if his sticks did not agree with his note, he held on to them and handed them over to his master at Canton.

This would appear to be a very primitive way of keeping an account, but it has always seemed to me a very correct one.

We were very soon discharged, and as we were what is termed 'off the letter,' we could not hope for a cargo of tea for London.

However, we took in one thousand chests for Singapore, and called in at Hong-Kong to take in more ballast.

We spent the third Christmas there, and arrived at Singapore by the middle of January 1844.

At Singapore we loaded for London, with antimony ore, terra japonica, pepper and rhubarb.

Singapore was a very pleasant place to load at, always a nice breeze through the day, and no mosquitoes at night, as we had at Whampoa and all up the Yang-tse-Kiang, added to which the good folks on shore were not in too great a hurry to send off the cargo, so the day's work was light.

We had no boating work to do, as there was a boat to attend on the ship.

The long boat, however, was out, and kept rigged, and on Sundays we went away in her and managed to pick up pine-apples and bananas enough to last the week ; also green cocoa-nuts.

The only drawback was the want of beef—we were fed on fresh pork and turtle. Of the latter we soon got tired.

There is a story told of the crew of a ship, that loaded at Singapore, complaining to the Lord Mayor of having been starved whilst lying in that port. His lordship inquired what kind of food had been given them. He was told turtle. His lordship said,—'Turtle ! turtle soup ! lots of green fat in it !' The answer was, 'Yes, large dollops as big as your fist ;' at which his lordship exclaimed,—'Lucky dogs! lucky dogs! I wish I had been there. Dismiss the case.' So poor Jack, as usual, got no sympathy.

However, we had rather fine times on the whole, and were sorry to leave, which we did at the end of March.

Our usual luck attended us; we made a very fair passage as far as St Helena, but got becalmed for twenty-eight days in the Sargarro Sea after losing the N.E. trades; fortunately we had plenty of fresh water, having filled up at St Helena.

But this was not the case with our companions in misfortune, of whom sixty-five could be counted from the masthead most days. Several of these had loaded with guano at the Island of Ichaboe, off the coast of Africa. All of them were short of water, and many of them of bread; nearly all of them had some of their crew down with fever, and went pulling about from ship to ship, begging water and asking for a doctor.

There was no doctor anywhere in the fleet, but as we had had great experience of this fever in China, and still had occasional cases, we were well up to the treatment, and fortunately had a good supply of quinine on board. The captain bought up a stock that had been sent out to China for sale, and which had arrived too late, as the expedition had broken up. This was sold at forty shillings the ounce (sea price).

Lying becalmed was very tiresome work, and the antimony ore in the bottom of the ship made her roll with a kind of pendulum motion, and all our sails got knocked to pieces, and when we did get a breeze it was a continual job of shifting and repairing.

We only arrived in London the end of July,

having been obliged to take steam when off Margate, as we had no more head sails.

Coming to an anchor off Margate on Sunday, we had the only accident of the passage.

A large sailing boat, full of men, women and children out for a sail, came too close to the ship, and whilst we were going astern, previous to letting go the anchor, got under the bow, and when the anchor was let go, the end of the stock caught the gunwale of the boat and capsized it, turning all the people into the water.

However, a good ducking was the only ill effects, and as our crew were overboard at once, with plenty of ropes' ends all were picked up and got on board, but the anchor had torn all the broadside out of the boat, so they had to remain on board till help came.

We had fine fun over getting the women's clothes dried. They and the children had to be kept in the cabin whilst the process was going on.

We were very glad to get to London, and so finish up a voyage which had lasted over three years, although we had nothing to complain of. I must say I have never forgotten the kindness I received from Captain William Broughton Pryce, Mr Alexr. Downie, the chief officer, and Mr Ed. Montgomery, the second officer, who were all first-rate officers and seamen, and who taught us lads our duty thoroughly, and took care we did it.

I have only come across the captain once since, and that was under adverse circumstances.

I was chief officer of the Royal Mail Steamer 'Thames,' bound from Southampton to North-fleet to be docked. We were stopped in the fog somewhere off Dungeness, and drifting about; presently we found ourselves close to a ship at anchor, and were hailed and given advice to come to an anchor as we were close in to Dungeness.

I recognised the voice of my old captain, and found the ship was the 'Walmer Castle,' under his command. Having got our exact position from him, we did not anchor but continued drifting up with the flood tide, and soon after the fog cleared. We were not, like the 'Walmer Castle,' dependent on wind, so kept on our way up.

CHAPTER IV.

HAVING finished up with 'La Belle Alliance,' the next thing to be done was to find another ship. This was no easy matter, as wherever I called and asked for employment, I was either told I was too young, or they said, 'If you had only looked in yesterday you were the very person we wanted.'

This state of things went on for some time, and I was beginning to think I was either born a day too late, or that it would have been better if I had not been born at all, when, through the kindness of Mr Wm. Shackell, then editor of the *John Bull*, I got an introduction to Captain Charles Mangles, one of the managers of the Royal Mail Steam Packet Company, which had started about two and a half years as contract-packets to carry the mails to the West Indies.

I called on that gentleman at the Company's office in Moorgate Street, and fortunately on what turned out to be the 'Right Day.'

They wanted a fourth officer for their ship the 'Tweed,' which was appointed to sail from Southampton on 17th October. Of course this ship could not get along without such an important appendage as a fourth officer, so there was no time to lose, that being the 14th of October.

Having examined the only two testimonials I had, the question was put,—'When could you join a ship?' I said,—'This evening, if the ship is in London,' which was considered satisfactory. I received the appointment, went to S. W. Silver & Company, and got some brass buttons put on my jackets and a gold band on my cap, and went down to Southampton and joined the 'Tweed' on 16th October, 1844.

The ship was moored in Southampton Water, a little above where Netley Hospital now stands. The 'Tweed' at that time was considered, and was, a large ship, being about 2400 tons register, and when I got on board I was considerably abroad. I entered by the starboard gangway port, which was on the main deck, and so strange was it to me that I was not at all sure which was forward and which was aft.

I was, however, received by the midshipman of the watch, and when I told him who I was, he soon let me know that I was the wrong man in the right place, as he had expected to be promoted himself, and, of course, abused me and the Company right off. Not finding this made any impression on me, as I had been used to be abused most of my life, he at length condescended to introduce me to the chief-officer, who seemed to be of a different opinion from Charlie Codd, the midshipman, and said he was glad the Company had filled up the berth with some one more likely to be of help to him than ' a brat of a midshipman.'

I found out, afterwards, that each of the three midshipmen on board had expected the appointment, and that they had been enemies to each other on that account for the last week or two. Now the matter was settled, and neither had got the berth, they joined forces against me. However, they soon found I was more than a match for them, added to which the chief and second officers received me well, finding that although I was young, I had had a good deal of hard experience.

The captain was an old Royal Naval officer and had been a master; his name was George Parsons, known in H.M. Service as Gentleman George (in contradistinction to his brother, Lieut. Jack, who had a different cognomen).

The captain took a liking to me from the time he saw me; he told me afterwards it was on account of what he was pleased to term my d—d cheek when I came on board.

My first introduction to him was at dinner in the saloon, the first day I joined. He put me to sit next to him, and made me quite at home.

I don't recollect any particular cheek at the time, and fancy he took to me more on account of my father having been a naval officer.

The first question he asked me was, who and what my father was, and when he found he had been in the R.N., and was dead, he extended the hand of fellowship to me at once, more especially as he had known him as harbour-master at Ramsgate when he put in there in H.M. brig 'Kestrel,' of which he had been second master in charge.

We sailed on 17th October, 1844, and were the first of the Royal Mail steamers that carried a hundred passengers from Southampton.

In those days the managers and some of the directors came down to see the ships off, and there was a grand luncheon served in the saloon, and free liquor; and there was, on that occasion, a good deal of speechifying on account of the hundred passengers which Captain, afterwards Admiral, Chappell, R.N., considered the turning-point of the Company's luck.

It would appear that a turning point for the better was much wanted, as they had lost several of their ships at the first start. This was not to be wondered at, as the ships were navigated without taking the deviation of the compass into consideration; in fact, in those days, very little was known about it. The course was always set by the starboard after-compass, notwithstanding there was frequently a point of difference between it and the port-one. There were only two compasses on deck, placed close to the steering wheel, which was right aft. It was not till three years after I joined that standard compasses were fixed in the ships, and even then they were seldom taken into consideration; they were, like the steering compasses, quite uncorrected, but they were fitted for taking azimuths, etc.

Having got fairly away and clear of the Needles passage, where the pilot left us, the routine of the ship commenced, and I found I was to keep the first watch with the third officer, one Mr Scott, whose whole experience at sea had been in the Royal Mail Service.

I soon found (except in steam-boat knowledge) I was a much better man than he, and I objected to the old quarter-master being appealed to on all occasions, as I found Mr Scott had been in the habit of doing. I had not been used to see the officer of the watch in charge of a nurse, and was not going to have it, as far as I was concerned, and it ended in my getting pretty well entire charge.

Nothing much turned up as far as Madeira ; we had a fine, fair wind, and carried sail all the way.

One night, as I was going round putting the lights out at eleven o'clock, a lady's maid stopped me and asked if I would go and speak to her mistress. I went to the cabin door, and found a stout, elderly lady, with a life-belt round her. At the best of times the cabin doorway was only about wide enough to allow her to go in and out, so what the object was in donning the life-belt I could not see, but it upset my gravity at once.

Being asked ' If the gale was abating ? ' did not tend to restore my equanimity, as we were going along with the topgallant-sail set to a fine, fair wind, and I laughed outright. The old lady said,—

' Young man, I did not send for you to laugh at me ; answer my question—Is the gale abating ? '

I told her there never had been any gale ; the weather was, and had been, quite fine. This did not pacify her, so she said,—

' Go away, young man ; I will report you to the captain as soon as I am well enough ; ' and so she did, much to the captain's amusement.

We remained at Madeira all one day, and all the passengers went ashore ; several were only go ing to Madeira for the winter. Amongst these was my friend (?) the heroine of the life-belt.

We left again with a fair wind, and next day sent up the studding-sail booms, and got the sails set. I now soon found out why the quarter-master had had so much to say in the watch—my friend Scott knew nothing about studding sails or, in fact, about any other sails. The boatswain's mate of the watch knew this, and took delight in appealing to him on various points which he felt sure would put his officer in a fix. He never got an answer till after the matter had been gone into by Scott and the quarter-master, who coached Scott and so enabled him to give the boatswain's mate the right order!

As Scott found I knew more than he did, he told the captain I would not obey his orders, so I was shifted into the chief-officer's watch, and had to keep from six to eight in the evening, and four to eight in the morning. The chief officer found I was well up to carrying on work, and made use of me accordingly.

When we were about half way down towards Barbadoes, there was a grand scrimmage in Scott's watch, and the ship had to be stopped for some hours.

The wind fell light, and it was necessary to trim sails as the steam was carrying the ship along faster than the wind was travelling. The wind had been just a little on the port quarter, the yards nearly square, and studding-sails set on both sides. Instead of friend Scott taking in his starboard studding-sails before trimming forward, he slacked off his port braces and forgot all about his lee studding-sail tacks ; the consequence was, the lee topmast studding-sail tack hooked on to one of the floats of the paddle wheel, and in much less time than it has taken to write it, wound down the topmast and topgallant studding-sail booms and the sails. The inside end of the top-mast studding-sail boom got in between two floats and forced itself up through the bottom of the starboard paddle-box boat—sails, gear and all being wound round the wheel.

The engineer of the watch, hearing a commotion in the wheel, and not knowing what it was, stopped his engines, and as soon as that took place, out turned everybody, passengers and all. It was rather difficult at first to make out what had happened. No one had ever seen a mast sticking up in the bottom of a paddle-box boat, and it was not till Scott, who had run right aft, was found, that any explanation could be given.

It was not till daylight that we could get to clear away the wreck, as the state of affairs in the paddle wheel was hopeless, even if we had been able to clear away the bulk of the mischief. Part of the gear had got wound round the outer end of the shaft, and till it was quite certain every bit was off, it would not have been advisable to go ahead again.

Having got over this little difficulty, we proceeded, and, without further mishap, arrived at Barbadoes on the twenty-first day after leaving Southampton.

The day before arrival there was a demonstration on the part of the passengers, at dinner-time, and, after a good deal of talk from one of them, a testimonial was sent to the captain, who took it in his hand and looked at it. When he found that it was only a paper testimonial, he got up and said,—

'Ladies and gentlemen, thirty years have I been an officer in H.M. Service, and I have not come here to ask a character from a parcel of "Travelling Tinkers." Take it back, waiter;' at the same time walking out of the saloon.

We never could find out any cause for this outbreak of indignation, but we concluded it arose from the fact of the passenger, who had done the talking and assumed the principal part in the transaction, being the proprietor of an ironmongery business in Trinidad.

At the time we arrived at Barbadoes, there was not much business going on, as it was not crop time, and the hurricane season had only just ended, so there were very few vessels in the port.

We lay there all day, transferring passengers and their baggage for Demerara to the R.M.S 'Dee,' which was waiting for them and the mail for British Guiana.

I was very much struck with the primitive-looking lighters, and the four negroes who manned each; out of the whole number that came along-side, I am certain there was not a single man that had on clothes that were not well patched, and I am sure that not a single man ceased talking all the time.

It was ludicrous to see the passengers being struggled for by the boatmen when they got to the foot of the gangway ladder, and to listen to the cries of 'See me here, sar; this boat the " Morning Star," sar;' ' In this boat the " Lady Ann," sar,' etc. I must say the Barbadoes boats and their crews are the best to be found anywhere in the West Indies, and the fares to and from the shore (one shilling per head) very reasonable, and only beaten at Malta, where the same distance in a boat costs only sixpence each; but the Barbadoes boatmen give you the extra sixpence in amusement as they go along.

Barbadoes is the only island in the West Indies where the negro is obliged either to work or starve, it is so thickly populated. At the time I am writing about it, it was the only island where the negroes were educated to any extent; in the whole course of my dealings with them, I have scarcely found one that could not read and write, and they have been taught thrift as well.

How this small island supports such a large population has always been a mystery to me; certainly, as I was told by one of the negroes to whom I was talking about it, 'the Lord sends plenty flying-fish, and several other kinds of fish;' he also said 'America sends flour and corn-meal, so there is always plenty to eat, and at the proper time the Lord opens the heavens and makes them all the same as a large watering-pot, so there is plenty to drink as well.'

These good people put more trust in the Lord (according to their own account) than any other people I have met.

At nightfall we left Barbadoes, and at about ten o'clock the next morning arrived at Grenada, the most beautiful of all the West Indian Islands. To my fancy, nothing can surpass the view which opens as Point Salines is rounded. I am not good at describing views. I must, therefore, suggest the reader should go and see it, and the lovely

harbour of St George's, the name of the port where
the steamers stop.

On arrival off the entrance, we were boarded by
Mr Martin, the harbour-master, who piloted the
ship in, and we were shortly moored to the two
jetties which constituted the coal-wharf, and the
work of coaling commenced.

This operation is carried on by coloured 'ladies'
(there are no women in the West Indies except
white women), who transport the coal in baskets
containing 80 lbs., on their heads, and march along
with it with a carriage that a countess might be
proud of, singing all the time. The men only fill
the baskets and lift them on to the ladies' heads.

In the harbour we found the R.M.S. 'Tay,' and
'City of Glasgow'—the former bound to Jamaica
and Mexico, the latter to Trinidad. We were
employed through the day transferring the
passengers, mails and baggage to them, and they
left at nightfall.

The great amusement of the day was the fussi-
ness of the three naval officers—old lieutenants—
over the transfer of the mails; one would have
thought there was a conspiracy on foot to rob the
bags, seeing that each of these old parties had his
sword on, to protect them if necessary.

It would also appear their education had been
neglected, by the number of mistakes that were

made in the accounts of the bags. One officer
had to furnish a list of the bags to the officer in
the other ship, keeping a duplicate, as he termed
it, 'for the information of the Lords Commissioners
of the Admiralty.'

The making out of these lists had taken the old
gentleman all the time he could spare from playing whist during the passage, and had it not been
for the second officer's help, I doubt if they would
have been ready in time!

At length all the mails were duly transferred,
and the time for mutual congratulations had
arrived—that is to say, drinks. Nothing in the
West Indies, any more than in England, being
put through satisfactorily without being kept
moist.

The two ships having been got off with the
usual amount of cheers, the next thing was for the
captain and the mail-agent to proceed to dine with
the officers of the garrison.

At that time there were white troops stationed
in every one of the islands. The ship's officers and
crew also went on shore. About eleven o'clock I, as
officer of the watch and expecting the return of
the captain and mail-agent, was told both of them
were locked up in the guard-room, by way of a
joke played on them by the soldiers.

It appeared that when they left the mess they

had not been furnished with the pass-word, and when they arrived at the first sentry, he would not let them go by without giving the word. The old agent, considering this an insult to H.M. Navy, showed fight, with the result that the sentry marched both him and the captain into the guard-room, where they were detained till a message was sent up to the barracks from the ship.

Of course there was a big row over this the next morning, which was not settled when we left.

CHAPTER V.

AT 6 A.M. on 10th November we left to do what was, and is, called the 'Northern Island' route. The first island we came to was St Vincent, a very picturesque little place, with a volcano of its own, and that is about all that can be said of it. We landed the mail there and started on, in about an hour, for St Lucia.

This island has a fine harbour, sheltered from nearly all winds, but at that time it was very unhealthy, and many deaths took place annually amongst the troops quartered there. It is also supposed to abound with snakes, but, in all my experience of the island, I have not heard of anyone being bitten. It was the custom to carry a small green snake in a bag round the neck, to keep off others. I was shown one of these by one Dr Blenderhasset, who embarked as a passenger. He was an inspector-general of hospitals, and a great collector of curiosities.

Several officers of the garrison came on board to see the doctor off—nominally, but actually to get iced drinks, as the steamer carried ice, but the shore did not boast of any. Ice-making machines were not invented at that time.

The next island was Martinique—a French one. I could not see much of it, as it was midnight when we arrived, and the ship stopped a long way off. I did not go ashore as there were no passengers to land, and my boat was not required. The mail-boat, only, went. It was close on daylight when it came back, the time having been taken up partly by the fuss made by the officials, and partly by the distance the boat had to pull.

Next in order came Dominica, of which we had fine views, as we had it before us more or less all day. Here we had nothing to land except the mail, but the captain went on shore to call on the governor, and it was past noon when we left. The officers of the garrison came off, and remained all the time the ship was there, giving them a slight change from the monotony of guard, etc. The ladies of the town of Roseau also paid us a visit, and I was a little astonished to find, although the island was English, the people, as a rule, spoke French.

Having left Roseau, we skirted along, the island

in good view, and at nightfall we passed Rupert's Bay, and soon left the island and got into a pretty rough sea. In a few hours more we got under the lee of the Saintes, some small islands to southward of Guadeloupe, and very soon arrived off La Basse-Terre Guadeloupe. We had several passengers for here, so my boat was called into requisition. We had not far to pull, and landed at the pier at 9 P.M. One passenger we brought had been cutting a big swell all the way along, and, of course, we thought he was some high official.

As he landed on the pier, he was met by his friends, all men, and we saw a lot of kissing going on between them. The purser and I followed him up the street, and, to our horror, we found our swell kept a shop, and the men who had been doing the kissing were his shopmen (called 'clerks' in the West Indies).

We only stayed about two hours at this place, and left before midnight for Antigua, where we arrived at breakfast time. We stopped off English Harbour, where the Royal Dockyard is situated. No one lived there but the dockyard officials and the garrison. The barracks were some distance up the hill, which looked into the harbour, called The Ridge, so we had no visitors, and only sent the mail boat on shore.

We were anxious to get away, as there were two islands to be called at that day—Nevis and St Kitts. We got to Nevis in good time, and to St Kitts at 5 P.M., as Nevis did not detain us long.

Here we had a lot of business to get through, as there were several officers, etc., to land with their baggage. One of these officers was a captain of Royal Engineers; he had been to England to get married and was arriving with his bride. Of course, as this lady was going ashore to be presented to every member of H.M. Service, it was necessary to get herself up for the occasion.

I must say she was very handsome, and beautifully dressed in fawn-coloured silk, with everything to match.

At that time there was no pier at Basse-Terre, and the landing was effected by beaching the boats. My boat, being heavily laden, took the ground well out, and a roller striking her turned her over, and we were all thrown out into the surf, and I saw the lovely fawn-coloured silk washing about in the mixture of sea water and black sand which skirted the so-called landing-place, and all the rest of her baggage likewise. So the poor lady not only landed wet through, but everything that composed her trousseau was wet and spoilt.

I was very sorry to see all this mischief, but it was no fault of mine. I laid my anchor out at the proper distance, but it did not hold in the sand and the boat was thrown on the beach. There is no doubt the boat was too heavily laden, but that was the chief officer's fault; it is a way chief-officers have of overloading one boat to save lowering another.

I have seen more accidents than one from this cause; of course I got the blame of it all, and was called a lubber when it was reported to the captain; fortunately the baggage was insured, so there was nothing to pay, or the Royal Mail Company would have known the value of a lady's trousseau.

The value of a passenger's trunk is never known till it is lost.

Towards the middle of the next day we passed through what is called the Round Island passage, and were in a kind of inland sea, called Drake's Channel, formed by several rocky islets on the south, and the island of Tartola on the north. Steaming over to the north side, we arrived off Road Town, the town of Tartola. Here I was dropped with the mail-agent in the mail-boat, and the steamer proceeded on to St Thomas, leaving us to do the business at Road Town and follow her down, as the captain was anxious to get into port and alongside the coal-wharf before dark.

Road Town was a very small place and also a very quaint one. The only official there was one

Dr Stobo. He was health officer, and questioned our sanitary condition before we landed. We then dealt with him as port-master, and found he was also the magistrate, island treasurer, tax collector, and chief of the police, and, as the president was away on leave, he was also 'acting president'; who after this would dare say that a Government official did not earn his salary?

Having got through the business at this important place, we started off (as the naval agent thought) to return to the ship, and when we got outside the bay, of course she was not to be seen. Before I left the ship the captain informed me he was going on, but cautioned me against telling the agent, or his plan would have been upset. I was therefore obliged to join with the agent in grumbling at having to sail twenty-three miles in the boat, which nevertheless was great enjoyment to me, as I was passionately fond of boat sailing.

We arrived safely alongside the ship in St Thomas Harbour in time for the saloon dinner, and only just in time. The row between the captain and the agent did not last long, and before dinner was over friendship between them was re-established. It is wonderful what can be done by a few glasses of wine in the way of settling quarrels.

We were occupied all the next day coaling, and

here was a new experience for me. I saw the ladies and gentlemen employed at the work were kept moving by a white man with a whip in his hands; the ladies also carried baskets on their heads which held 112 lbs. coal, instead of 80 lbs. as at Grenada, and had to move smartly with their load, or the whip came into requisition.

At first I did not understand this, but, on inquiry, found these ladies and gentlemen were slaves hired from their owners by Mr Stubbs, who had the contract for coaling the steamers.

Slavery had been abolished twelve years in the English Islands, but was still in force in the Danish and Spanish. We did not get coaled any quicker here than we did at Grenada, if so quickly, and it was a sorry sight to see women driven like cattle.

We only remained at St Thomas one day and two nights, as we were bound to Bermuda to meet the homeward-bound mail-steamer and hand over all the mails for Europe we had picked up since leaving Barbadoes.

Before we left, the R.M.S. ' Medway ' arrived, having brought the mails from Jamaica, Hayti and Porto Rico, which were transferred to our ship; they also brought along the captain, officers and crew of the Royal Mail Company's steamer ' Actæon,' which had lately been wrecked on Point Canoas, near to Carthagena on the Spanish Main.

This vessel was thrown away (I can't call it anything else) at about 9.30 A.M., in beautiful clear weather. The captain and all the officers having left the deck to go down to breakfast, the ship was left in charge of the quarter-master, whose orders were ' to keep Point Canoas on with the fore-rigging.' He would appear to have carried out his orders most implicitly, as the ship ran ashore going full speed, and there was not one eighth of a mile between the point and the fore-rigging and a good-sized hole in her bottom, right underneath it; fortunately the wind was off the land and the water quite smooth, so the loss of a beautiful ship was the only result of this gross misconduct.

On the sixth day from St Thomas we arrived at Bermuda, having made the light on Gibb's Hill about 10 P.M. the night before; we found the R.M.S. 'Avon' from Mexico, Havana and Nassau in the Camber at Ireland Island, where the dockyard was situated. The mails for Bermuda we had previously landed at St George's Island.

I had a letter of introduction to Captain Strutt, R.N., who was in command of the 'Avon,' and invited me to breakfast the next day. We of the 'Tweed' did not think much of the 'Avon,' as there seemed to be a general misunderstanding between every one on board, resulting in a general clear out when the ship arrived home.

There were always great complaints of the diet, and the day before the ship arrived at Southampton, one of the passengers wound up the usual speech made in the saloon with the doggerel :—
' Between

> Pork hot and pork cold,
> Pork tender and pork tough,

Thankee, Strutt, we have not had enough, except of you and the pork.'

I was very much amused at the black pilot who took the ship in ; his sense of importance was quite worthy a newly-made Lord Mayor, but I must say he seemed well up to his business, and piloted the ship safely through the exceedingly intricate channel.

The ' Avon ' having sailed, we were able to complete our stock of coal. This we did by hoisting in sacks from lighters, a very tedious business at that time, as steam winches were not the order of the day, and we were only supposed to take in one hundred tons a day. We also took in a good supply of holystone and sand.

The sailors used to say of Bermuda, it had three crops a year—one of holystone and two of sand !

The next place we visited was Nassau, New Providence, which was then a very small town, but which has since developed into a fashionable winter resort for Americans. We arrived off Hog Island

Light and anchored at 4 A.M. on the fourth day from Bermuda, and remained till evening.

Very little was doing ashore, and the inhabitants appeared to be happy and contented; children abounded, and mostly amused themselves playing in the water, which was as clear as glass and of a beautiful blue colour. You could see to the bottom of the harbour, and it was studded here and there with sea-fans and anemones.

Some ladies employed themselves in making shell-baskets, flowers, and ornaments, otherwise the place seemed to produce nothing and was totally uninteresting.

We passed through the Bahama Channel, and in due course arrived at Havana, the only place of any importance to which we had been. The approach is very beautiful (though not equal to St George's, Grenada) and the harbour perfect. The eastern part of it is sheltered from all winds, and a large fleet can be accommodated. There is one shoal on the south side, called the Reglia, but it is no detriment to the port.

Slavery still existed, and the British cruisers were very active all round the island, endeavouring to prevent any more slaves being landed.

H.M.S. 'Rodney' was moored in the harbour as a receiving ship for the negroes found on board the slavers, which the cruisers took from time to time, and these were denominated 'Emancipados, as they were free immediately they got on board one of H.M. ships.

H.M. schooner 'Pickle' had captured a vessel with over three hundred men and women on board, a fortnight before we arrived, and these people were to be sent to Jamaica. They were put on board our ship for the purpose when we were ready to start, and a fine time out we had with them. We were six days going to Jamaica, and several births took place on the passage.

We were very glad when we got rid of these savages. They had scarcely any clothes, and nothing to lie on but coarse mats made of rushes. It took us a full week to get the ship clean, and it was very much longer before she was sweet again. Fortunately, Jamaica furnishes plenty of fresh water, and, after we had completed the coal, we took full advantage of the supply which was brought down to the end of the Company's wharf.

The name of the island is derived from its water supply. It was, in the time of the Spaniards, called Xamaica, or the Land of Springs.

Jamaica is a splendid island, and, notwithstanding the general idea of yellow fever entertained of it in England, it has a most beautiful climate, particularly in the higher parts.

I have known people who have gone there with

only one lung (and that not too good an one), live and enjoy good health for years.

People are apt to judge Jamaica by Kingston—the place where they land from the steamships that bring them—and so form a very bad idea of the whole island.

Kingston is certainly a very poor specimen of a city, and does not appear to be at unity with itself. Each inhabitant that builds a house regulates the height of the pavement in front of it, and, as you walk along, except you keep in the roadway, you have to go up and down steps.

At the time of which I am writing, the streets were not lighted, and it was necessary to carry a lantern after dark. Now, they not only have gas, but also the electric light; but the irregularity of the pavement still remains.

It is difficult to understand why Jamaica does not go ahead; but, to my mind, it does not; and I am of opinion that it never will, till more white folks are induced to settle in it.

There are thousands and thousands of acres of land on which white agricultural-labourers could work and live, and fare better than in such regions as Argentina and the Banda Orientale Republic, where they have to learn a new language, and find, mostly, a different religion from their own.

Jamaica is well provided with schools for children, and presents all the advantages that can be found in England; and to these are added a beautiful climate, a fertile soil, and land for sale at a low price. There are churches and places of worship of every denomination, great security of life and property, and, in fact, everything that a poor man can want is to be found there, except public-houses and gin-palaces, which are the inventions of those whose interest it is to keep the poor man poor. Consequently, he would improve his condition by going to a country where there are none of them.

We remained a week at Kingston, Jamaica, and then started with the homeward mail, which we were to carry as far as St Thomas.

Leaving Kingston at 8 A.M., we arrived the next afternoon at Jacmel, a town on south side of Hayti, which is a ' Black Republic.'

The island of St Domingo is divided into two republics — the western is called Hayti, and the eastern retains the name of St Domingo; in the former the language is French and in the latter Spanish. With the latter I have not had any communication.

At Jacmel the anchorage is very limited, but quite sufficient for the traffic, so we only laid off, and sent the boat ashore for and with the mail.

As the sea breeze was blowing, and pretty strong, the steamer stopped far out, allowing the boat to sail in. By the time it had done its business on shore, the steamer had drifted within a reasonable distance, and the breeze began to take off, so the boat had no difficulty in reaching to the ship again.

The next business was to look out for the Rocky Islet, called Alto Telo in Columbus's voyages, seventy miles S.E. from Jacmel. We passed it in the middle watch and then hauled up to the eastward, having a chart to navigate by, which carried the statement—'this part of the coast imperfectly surveyed;' so we gave the shore a wide berth and saw nothing of it till we got well over to the island of Porto Rico, when we hauled up and passed through the Mona Channel, between St Domingo and Porto Rico, arriving in due course at the city of San Juan, Porto Rico.

This is another fine harbour, but only fit for vessels of light draught, as there is not too much water on the bar at the entrance. We did not go in with the ship, as the boat could do all the work required. It had a long way to go, and only got back at 8 P.M. The sea was pretty high alongside the ship, and we had a good deal of difficulty in getting the boat hooked on and hoisted.

The next morning we arrived at St Thomas,

found there the 'Severn' bound to Bermuda, to which ship we turned over the mail for Europe, and then proceeded on the return Northern-Island-route to Grenada, from whence we went to Barbadoes and Demerara, calling at Tobago on the way.

This is considered more likely to have been the scene of Robinson Crusoe's abode than Juan Fernandez, inasmuch as from Juan Fernandez what is described as the mainland could not have been seen, whereas from Tobago, at the south-west end the land can plainly be seen, and the passage is such that canoes can easily go to and fro.

We called in at Great Courland Bay and landed the mail, but did not go to Scarboro, the chief town of the island. Nothing was moving at Tobago, and it appeared very little more lively than at the time of Robinson Crusoe. I have not been there for years, but fancy, from the accounts I hear, it still remains in the same state.

Thirty-six hours from Tobago brought us to Demerara, and we moored off the Market Stelling at George Town. Here we found more life and business; at least thirty vessels were at anchor, and sugar-making was going on.

Guiana is not troubled with hurricanes, and sugar-making goes on nearly the whole year. This colony has great advantages over the West

India Islands, where sugar can only be made from the end of January to July, as everything is supposed to be shipped, and the ships away by the first week of August, or double insurance has to be paid.

The machinery also is usually idle from July to the next January, hence it does not pay as well there to have it as it does in Guiana.

We remained at George Town five days, and passed New Year's day there.

The captain had a table rigged on the quarter-deck and invited the officers, engineers, and warrant-officers to see the old year out, and the new year in.

As I had the morning watch, I was excluded from this entertainment. I was supposed to be called at 4 A.M. However, I slept on till daylight (not having been called), and wondered that everything was so still on board, as the hands should have been mustered at 5-30; also, as we were to sail that afternoon at tide-time, there should have been some stir in the boiler-room.

I turned-out and went on deck, and found the quarter-deck party still there, sound asleep—quarter-masters included.

I succeeded in waking up the captain and got him down to his cabin, and after that woke up the rest of them and made the boatswain turn the hands out before I let him go to lie down, so we got to work soon after six. The engineers picked themselves up bravely and made a start with their men, getting up steam, and by eight o'clock we had got the New Year fairly started—that is to say, every one on board had recovered the hard work of the previous night, and we were ready to unmoor at slack-water. One anchor was stowed by noon, so no great harm was done, and, as the crew observed, the 'pot could not call the kettle black.'

The tide served for leaving at 4 P.M., and we got over the bar and dropped the pilot at the lightship in good daylight. This bar is a great drawback to Demerara, as only ships of a comparatively light draught can load inside, and it costs more than the freight is worth to finish loading outside, where there is always considerable swell on.

It is, however, a great thing for the Royal Mail Company, as it prevents large steamers going there.

The Demerara folks are always threatening to have a line of their own, and at one time induced the Cunard Company to build some vessels expressly for the purpose of running in opposition to the Royal Mail.

But these good people soon found that the Demerara folk's swans were only geese, and they gave up running there.

I have never been able to understand why the bar has been allowed to remain in such condition as to interfere with the trade of the port. There is no reason why it should, except it is for the benefit of the party who has the monopoly of the Coastal Steam Navigation, and reaps a harvest from towing ships.

If the colony would only have a powerful tug of its own, using it as a dredger, during the ebb-tide, and to tow ships, the expense of it would be covered by the towing, the price of which should be included in the pilotage; the bar would soon cease to be a trouble, particularly if a narrow channel were buoyed off and all screw-steamers were taken by the pilots through it.

There is no dredger so effectual as a screw-steamer! When screw steamers commenced running to Kingston, Jamaica, there were only five fathoms water in the channel off Fort Augusta, now there are six and a-half and seven fathoms.

There certainly is a great difference in the size of the steamers that go to Kingston, as well as in the number, but I am firmly of opinion that, in a few years, if my idea were carried out, the largest steamers likely to be employed in the West India trade would be able to go in and out the Demerara River.

We called at Courland Bay, Tobago, on our return passage, thence went on to Grenada, and waited for the next outward mail from England, the Jamaica portion of which we were to carry to that island, and the Haytian portion to Jacmel.

We duly arrived off the Royal Mail Wharf at Kingston and found a very strong sea-breeze blowing, the captain being over-careful getting alongside, some time elapsed before the mail was landed. The wharf was, as usual, crowded with people, who began to get impatient at standing there so long in the coal-dust. One gentleman called out,—'I wonder, captain, you don't land the mail.' This, of course, did not please the captain, and he called out,—'Wonder, sir! you should never wonder till a crow builds her nest inside of you, and then you can wonder how she got the sticks there!'

This sally turned the grumbling of the crowd into laughing, and before another change came over them we were alongside.

Amongst the passengers to be landed was a very fair young lady, newly married to a coloured gentleman, whose parents were on the wharf to receive them. His mother was nearly black, and she made a rush at her newly-arrived daughter-in-law, and tried to kiss her; but this was too much for the young lady, and 'mamma' was greeted by a slap in the face. The husband said,—'My dear Sophy, how could you treat my mother so?' To which the young lady retorted,—'How was I to know that black woman was your mother? If I had thought such a thing, I would never have married you; as it is I shall return to England by the next mail if these are the aristocratic relations you told me of.' And back she did go in our ship.

I suppose the coloured gentleman had forgotten to say that his mother's relations were chiefly living in Africa, and that the good lady herself was born in a slave cabin on one of the estates in Jamaica, having been reckoned a slave till the last twelve years, and that he, in fact, had been in the same category, although sent to England and brought up as a barrister!

In due course we left Kingston for England, *via* Jacmel, Porto Rico and St Thomas, calling at Fayal (Azores) on the way; we had, when we left Jamaica, a strong trade wind to go against, and the same after passing St Thomas; this was followed up by strong east winds, which lasted till we got home. We should have taken some coal at

Fayal, but the weather would not allow it, so we had what is called the 'coal-fever' badly towards the latter part of the passage, and, as we did not carry cargo, the ship was very top-heavy by the time we arrived at Southampton.

However, we got there, and that was considered somewhat of a triumph in those days, though I think the chief engineer would have collapsed if we had been a couple of days longer at sea.

We remained at Southampton for close on six weeks, sailing again on 17th April, 1845. Great changes took place in the ship's officers during this time; Mr Scott, the chief-officer, had to leave, as he had made an imprudent marriage; Mr Moss, the second officer, was promoted to be chief officer of the 'Medway'; Mr Scott, who had been third, was left out in the West Indies as chief-officer of the R.M. schooner 'Liffey,' which had been put on the Spanish-Main-route after the loss of the 'Actæon'; Mr Codd, the senior midshipman, was made fourth officer of the 'Dee'; Mr Ellison joined as chief-officer, Mr Onslow as second, and Mr Keys as third.

I had expected the latter appointment, as I had been acting since leaving Jamaica, but was considered 'too young.'

This change of officers was very much for the better in every way; the new chief was a smart officer, and very soon got the ship into such order as pleased the captain and the crew as well. Sailors, as a rule, don't like a slack ship; and the officers were company for one another, which is always a great thing; we had a fine fellow for purser, Mr John Ballard, and not such a bad sort of a surgeon, Stephen Troome, M.D., a west country-man, one of the old school, who took quantities of snuff, a large reserve of which he carried loose in his right-hand waistcoat pocket.

We had very few passengers on the outward passage, and went exactly the same route as we did on the previous voyage.

One evening we were calling at St Pierre, Martinique, and I was on shore with the purser, the second officer being, also, ashore, with the Ad-miralty agent. There was some delay on the part of the P.O. folks about the mail, and we had to wait a little, so we took the opportunity of look-ing in at the billiard-room near the landing-place, where were several French officers playing. Our purser criticising their play gave offence, with the result that one officer challenged him to play for a doubloon (64s.) on the game; this unfortunate man soon found he had never made a greater mistake in his life, as Jack Ballard was one of the best billiard players I knew; in fact, before start-ing in the purser line, he had made his living by billiards, which he had played in most, if not all, of the capitals in Europe.

The officer's doubloon was very soon in Jack's pocket.

This did not improve the condition of affairs, and by way of what the officers considered an insult, they challenged him to play the marker.

Friend Ballard was equal to the occasion, and with his usual *sang-froid* replied, in the best of French,—

'It is a little *infra dig.* for a gentleman to play with a marker, but, at the same time, if he is the only person you consider a match for me, I don't mind, only it must be for five doubloons.'

After considerable chattering between the officers and the marker, which both Ballard and myself understood, it was agreed to, and the money lodged with the proprietor of the rooms.

The marker had the first start and made a break after a few strokes.

The purser then took the table and played the game out without a break, and so won the five doubloons—equal to £16.

I was unable to see the finish, as the second officer sent me down to the landing-place to bring along three men out of the mail boat and five men out of mine, with the boat's stretchers, in case there should be any row over the money; but when we arrived up we found the purser and second officer leaving the rooms amid the cheers of the French officers, who were well satisfied at the defeat of the marker and with the jovial manner of our worthy purser.

In due course we left Jamaica for home, *via* St Thomas, as, before, with a considerable number of passengers, one of whom I had a narrow escape from shooting.

As we were going through the Mona Channel, between St Domingo and Porto Rico, there were a large number of birds called 'boobies' flying about the ship, and I went into the purser's cabin, situated on the half-deck just abaft the starboard-gangway-port, and loaded his pistols with a view to having a shot at the boobies; somehow, one of them went off, the ball passing through the bulk-head, between the heads of two ladies who were seated just outside, the one resting her head on the shoulder of the other.

Of course they heard the noise, but I was sharp enough to whip the cork out of a large Eau de Cologne bottle, and plug the hole up with it; having done this I bolted, and it was some days before the ladies, or anyone else, knew what had happened.

After everything was quiet for the night, I got some putty from the carpenter, made the hole good, and gave the place a rub of paint.

We got a large increase in the number of passengers at St Thomas, and had a pleasant passage home, calling at Fayal on the way.

We arrived off Fayal about 8 A.M. on the fourteenth day from St Thomas, and as the weather was fine I was sent on shore with the purser to bring off supplies.

Just at that time there was a good deal of excitement over an American doctor (I think his name was Webster) who had murdered a Dr Parkman, cutting up the body and burning it piecemeal in his study fire.

Before leaving St Thomas we had learnt that he had been hanged. When we got to the landing-place, we were met by several people, amongst whom were the United States Consul and his wife. This young lady was, in some way, related to Dr Webster.

The consul asked me if there was any news, and I, not knowing there was any connection between his family and Dr Webster, said 'all the news was that they had hung that scoundrel Webster;' on which the poor lady collapsed.

By the time the purser had got the supplies together, amongst which was a live bullock, the ship had drifted well over towards the opposite island, Pico, so I got sail on the boat and, with the bullock in tow, started off towards her.

When I was about mid-channel, the ship began to move towards Fayal again. Whether the captain did not see me, or for any other reason, I don't know, though she passed us close she did not stop to take us on board, and we had to get the boat round and go back after her. Fortunately the wind was what is called a ' soldier's wind,' and we were enabled to sail, or I don't know when we should have fetched her.

When I got on board, instead of receiving any commiseration, the captain inquired,—' Why the devil I had not waited till the ship closed in for me, instead of starting after her like a lunatic?' so you see zeal is not always commendable.

The passengers amused themselves whilst the ship lay to by buying fruit and baskets, which were brought alongside in boats, and as the purser had brought off a good supply of fruit, we had any amount during the remainder of the passage. We did not want any coal at Fayal, so, as soon as my boat was cleared and hoisted, we resumed our voyage, arriving at Southampton on the twentieth day after leaving St Thomas.

CHAPTER VI.

WE did not remain many days at Southampton, as the ship required docking, and there was no dry-dock there.

We accordingly went up to London and were placed in Messrs Wigram's dock at Blackwall. Steamships of the size of the 'Tweed' were still considered worth visiting, and we had many visits from first-class people, and one midshipman was told off each day to conduct them round the ship.

One day a very nice-looking midshipman had this duty, and a lady, as she went away, offered him a sovereign, to the great indignation of the young man, who refused it.

The lady said,—

'Pack of nonsense! I know very well a sovereign is *always* acceptable to a young fellow like you! I have boys of my own; take it, and don't be a fool.'

He was wise enough to take the lady's advice and the sovereign.

I was not allowed to remain long idle, for I was promoted to be third officer of the 'Medway,' and had to return to Southampton to join her.

The 'Medway' was commanded by Captain Andrews, a much younger man than the captain of the 'Tweed.' He must have got in by strong interest, for he had seen very little sea service, and that only in yachts, and was about as well fitted to command a ship like the 'Medway,' as I was to be Archbishop of Canterbury.

It was fortunate he had such a chief officer to nurse him as Mr Moss. The second officer was an old sea-dog, Stoddart by name; he had but one eye, and if only trouble had been taken to reckon up from his yarns the time he had put in at sea, I should say he must have first started with Noah. He went by the name, on board, of Boreas Albin, who is said, by sailors, to have been chief-mate of the Ark!

We sailed from Southampton on 2d September, and so went on a different route. We arrived at Barbadoes in due course, went on to Grenada, and along the Northern Islands, and to Porto Rico, returning to Grenada, Barbadoes, Demerara, and back to Grenada, from whence we went on to Jamaica, Havana, Vera Cruz and Tampico.

In this connection I will mention a curious circumstance that nearly had a tragical end.

The steward of the ship was a Dutchman, Julius Price by name. In those days the meat and fish for the outward passage was mostly carried in ice, and stowed for each day's consumption.

This was taken out of the ice-house at 9.30 A.M. daily by the butcher and chief-steward.

One morning there was a difference of opinion between the steward and the butcher, the latter being inside the ice-room.

The altercation getting stronger, the steward said to the butcher,—'I shall not put up with this!' thereupon he shut the door to, locked it and went away, leaving the butcher inside!

The steward must have forgotten all about this occurrence, and it was not till the butcher was wanted in the afternoon, at 3.30, to give water to the sheep, that he was missed, and a hunt made for him, when it was generally supposed he had gone overboard.

The steward now recollected that he had left him locked up, and exclaimed,—

'Mine Gott! I has left him in the ice-house, this morning.'

It was fortunate this had been discovered, for, if the man had been left much longer, he would have died.

As it was, it took all the doctor knew to bring him to, after having been $5\frac{1}{2}$ hours in the intense cold and in a place almost air-tight.

The steward, fearing the consequences, left the ship at St Thomas, and settled there as a store-keeper.

The route we had taken was called the Mexican route, and was by far the most lucrative for the captain.

We were expecting to arrive at Vera Cruz early one morning, and made the Light about midnight, but it came on to blow a norther, and we had to remain off the port for five days, the harbour of Vera Cruz being open to the north.

We were not too comfortable during this time, as we had one thousand bottles of quicksilver on the main-deck, ready to be landed at Vera Cruz for use in the silver mines. These required constant watching to prevent them fetching away, and we were very glad when we were able to get into port and be rid of them ; they also made the ship roll badly.

Having finished at Vera Cruz, we went up the coast to Tampico, and found that a conductor had just arrived with three millions of dollars for shipment to the Bank of England by our ship.

We lay at some distance outside the bar, and the

town of Tampico being some distance up the river, the process of shipment was rather tedious; it all had to be done in launches, rowed off by sixteen men, and hoisted in nets, six bags in each, containing 3000 dollars in a loose-matted bag, through the meshes of which the silver was plainly visible. It had travelled in these bags on mule-back all the way from the mines, and it was a wonder to me a lot of it had not been lost. Each bag was weighed as we received it, and then stowed in the bullion-room.

The freight on this treasure was 2½ per cent. at that time, and the captain got 2½ per cent. on the 2 per cent., as his share, which, for this shipment, would amount to £150.

We called in at Vera Cruz after leaving Tampico, took in some more treasure, and fourteen passengers, of whom ten composed the family of a French doctor, and four a party who had been travelling in Mexico—viz., two guardsmen and their two soldier-servants.

The whole party had come down from the city of Mexico in the diligence, and, as the officers observed, by good luck, the conveyance had been attacked by brigands. The brigands made a mistake on this occasion, as the doctor shot the gentleman who came to the right-hand window, and his son shot the gentleman who came to the left-hand window. The officers and their servants dropped four others with their rifles from the top of the coach, and this, added to the fire from the conductor's blunderbuss, dispersed the party, and the diligence arrived at Vera Cruz without further molestation.

I afterwards met the two officers in the Crimea —one was quarter-master general, the other, poor fellow, was killed at Inkerman.

Leaving Vera Cruz we steamed up the coast and anchored off a place called Rio Antigua, it having been arranged between General Sta. Anna (who had been and was, up to that time, Dictator of Mexico) and the captain, to call off there and take the general and his belongings on board, on the quiet, as he found the country was getting too warm for him.

The captain was to get 15,000 dollars for this service, equal to about £3020.

We anchored there at daylight in the morning, and sent the boats on shore. Everything was ready ; we took all into the boats, got them on board, and left by eight o'clock.

The captain went ashore in his gig, and brought off the General and Madame Sta. Anna, and his 15,000 dollars with them.

In the general's baggage there were packed 300,000 dollars in Mexican doubloons.

We now went to Havana, and thence to Nassau and Bermuda.

Here we coaled and received the mails and passengers for home from the ' Tweed,' and started for England.

Whilst at Bermuda we had an *émeute* with the engineers of the two ships ; those from the ' Tweed ' had come on board our ship and joined our engineers in a convivial in the engineers' mess-room.

The dockyard regulations required all lights to be out on board at 10 P.M., and I, as officer of the watch, had to see this regulation carried out. When I arrived at the mess-room door, the engineers refused to put their light out, and I was obliged to refer the matter to the captain. He ordered me to call the chief officer and tell him to clear the ship of the ' Tweed's ' engineers at once, and have the light put out. The engineers were in a fighting state, and we had to clear them out on to the quay by force, where the dockyard-guard took charge of them, and confined them in the guard-room. Our engineers turned in, and this ended the business for the time.

We had a tolerably rough passage between Nassau and Bermuda, and I had my first experience of a hurricane. Lieut.-Col. Reid (afterwards Sir Wm. Reid) happened to be on board, and instructed us in his theory of the 'Law of Storms,' and as it was illustrated at the same time, I thoroughly understood it, and have acted upon the knowledge then gained on all needful occasions since, with the greatest success.

On the passage home we had some little amusement with a Baptist minister, who, with his wife and three small children, were passengers.

The captain was simple enough to allow this minister to conduct the service on Sunday, with the result that might have been expected, as he was the only Baptist on board.

Towards the conclusion, he and his wife and little folks started a hymn, and the crew attempted to join in. Presently the good wife showed symptoms of discomfiture, and, finally, was very seasick, to the great amusement of all present, except themselves. The captain was obliged to give the order to pipe down, and get the saloon cleared.

That evening Mr Minister had rather more to drink than was good for him, and went about the fore-end of the ship rousing up the watch by calling out, 'Get up! get up and reef the main-sail!' Jack does not like being disturbed unnecessarily, and resented the interference by giving the minister what they termed a 'baptising in sea water.' This being reported to the captain in the morning, the verdict was given,—'Sarved him right.'

After our arrival at Southampton, the *émeute* at Bermuda was the subject of an investigation, and as engineers in those days were more scarce than they are now, the blame was put on me, and I was transferred from the 'Medway' to the 'Avon,' which ship was in the Southampton Dock getting new boilers.

I was very glad to leave the 'Medway,' as I did not like the captain, and he did not like me. The only regret I had was leaving my messmate and friend, Oliver Cromwell Field, who was the second officer. He was a good one, and a very amusing man. On one occasion we had cold fowl for tea in the mess-room, and no ham was sent up with it. He ordered the servant down to the head steward with his compliments, and, 'Did he think we were cannibals, to eat chicken without ham?'

It being winter time, living on board a ship with all the middle section open was not too comfortable, and we were very glad to get to sea again, which we did on 17th February, 1847, and went the usual route, as far as Havana. There we found the officers and crew of the 'Tweed,' which ship had been wrecked on the Alecrans, a reef between Havana and Vera Cruz, on the 12th February, at 3.30 A.M.

We received them all on board, and left for Nassau and St Thomas. We lost a day on the passage, through mistaking a new light which had been placed on Cuba for the Double Headshot Cag Light. The mistake was not discovered till we got the latitude at noon the next day, and we had to retrace our course; so our shipwrecked friends narrowly escaped a second mishap.

This delay prevented us catching the 'Tay' at St Thomas as we expected.

We fell in with the 'Eagle,' bound from St Thomas to Porto Rico, thirty miles to westward of St Thomas, and received information that the 'Tay' had left for Bermuda at 6 P.M. that day, so as there was no use in our going on to St Thomas, we altered our course and went in chase of the 'Tay.'

Fortunately that vessel had lost her bearings in the night, and was obliged to stop for four hours, which gave us the chance of coming up with her, as we did at 8 A.M. the next day.

All the mails, passengers, etc., which the 'Tay' had for England, were transferred to us by means of the paddle-box boats of the two ships, without the slightest trouble or accident, and we parted company at nightfall, the 'Tay' shaping her course for Nassau and Havana, and our ship for Bermuda and Southampton.

This transfer of valuable goods at sea recurred to my mind when, in later years, the country was put to the expense of sending a squadron of men-of-war to the Western Ocean to find out if it were possible to transfer coal to them at sea from coal ships.

An account of the loss of the 'Tweed' will be found at the end of Part I., page 139.

I went another voyage in the 'Avon,' and then joined the 'Forth' as acting-second-officer, to proceed to the West Indies and exchange into the 'Conway' as second officer.

The 'Forth' was commanded by Lieutenant Chapman, R.N., a gentleman very much of the old school, but a highly-efficient officer, nevertheless. He was the most vigilant man I have ever been with at sea, and the officer of the watch never knew when he might find the old man close behind him looking over his shoulder to see if he were asleep.

By way of averting such a catastrophe, we were made to carry a very large night-glass, about two feet long, and four inches in diameter. This we called 'Laura,' after the shorter of the captain's two daughters. In the daytime the old gentleman carried about with him, when on deck, a telescope, three feet six inches long. This we called 'Bessie,' after the other Miss Chapman, who was long and thin.

The captain was very particular about the

quarter-deck, and did not like to see the marks of the nails in the passengers' boots on it, so it was, therefore, the business of the ship's joiner to attend in the morning whilst the Boots was at work, and pull all the nails out of the offending soles. India-rubber soles were not yet invented.

We had a very stout passenger on board belonging to Jamaica. This gentleman travelled with a large easy-chair, in which he sat on deck, and was wheeled along when it was necessary to move him.

One afternoon, when the captain came on deck, the operation of moving this gentleman had just been carried out, and the deck showed the marks of the castors. It was my watch, and I was sent for, and got well scolded for allowing it; more row could not have been made of it if I had run a vessel down.

To see this old skipper taking the sun was quite a sight. He used an old-fashioned quadrant, strapped together by marline, and set up with lead pencils, and held a watch, $2\frac{1}{2}$ inches in diameter, in his left hand. This had a lanyard of log-line, with which he made it fast to his arm; as soon as he had taken the sun's altitude, he took the time by the watch, then let it go, and whilst he read off the altitude and marked it and the time in the book which he held in his teeth with the pencil in it, the watch was swinging by its lanyard!

On arrival at Grenada, I joined the 'Conway' as second-officer. This was a newly-built vessel, originally designed for a Trinity House lightship, lengthened by the bow, and turned into a steam vessel. She was very strong, but not neat (and answered to the sailor's simile of an old woman's cap served up with a jack-chain). Her speed at the best was ten knots per hour.

I remained in this vessel, employed on the Northern Island and Demerara routes, till she returned to England in May 1848, and had generally a good time, becoming well known to everyone along the line, all of whom were most hospitable and friendly.

I next joined the 'Trent,' famous in after years as the vessel from which Messrs Slidell and Mason, the U.S. Confederate Commissioners, were taken by Captain Wilkes of the U.S. frigate 'San Jacinto' in 1861, which act very nearly caused war between England and the United States.

In this 'Trent' we were kept constantly in a state of excitement — the captain, Clarke by name, an old East India Company's officer, holding a court of inquiry on one thing or another most mornings.

He had left off going to sea for some tim

before he joined the Royal Mail Company, and had been a magistrate and a churchwarden. He always went by the latter name in the service, and if he had been as much trouble to the parson as he was to us, I have no doubt the parson was glad when he went to sea out of his way, as he would probably have wanted the church carried on in ship-shape fashion.

I will relate one inquiry, which will show what others were like.

The captain liked a hot kidney for his luncheon, but so did the purser, and the latter being in more favour with the butcher and cook, got all the kidneys, notwithstanding the orders of the captain.

Hence an inquiry into this was held, with the result that the butcher succeeded in making the captain believe that the sheep supplied on that voyage had no kidneys. The butcher also said,—

'If you don't believe me, sir, the next time I kill a sheep you had better come and see for yourself.'

Accordingly, the next evening the captain, attended by the purser as witness, went to see the sheep killed, when, lo and behold! that sheep certainly appeared to have no kidneys. The captain was so satisfied that, on arrival at Southampton, he found fault with the people who supplied the sheep, on 'account of their being without kidneys'! They seemed to accept the fact as related, but suggested another butcher being engaged for the ensuing voyage.

From the 'Trent' I was transferred to the 'Thames,' and went one trip only in her. After that I was promoted to be chief officer of my old ship, the 'Conway,' to join which I was sent out as passenger in the 'Medway,' Captain W. Seymour, afterwards lost in the R.M.S. 'Amazon,' which was burnt at sea on the night of 4th January, after leaving Southampton, a new ship, on 2nd January, 1852.

I served in the 'Conway' as chief officer from September 1850 till September 1851, when I was invalided and took passage home in the 'Avon.'

I arrived home in time to pass the last two days of the Great Exhibition of 1851 in viewing it, being sufficiently restored to enable me to do so.

I was next appointed chief-officer of the ill-fated 'Amazon,' then fitting out at Blackwall; but, fortunately for me, something went wrong with the chief-officer of the 'Great Western,' which ship was to sail on 17th December, and I was at the last moment taken out of the 'Amazon' and sent down to Southampton to take his place.

In the early part of 1852, an epidemic of yellow fever broke out in the West Indies, and the crews of the mail steamers suffered very much, several officers died and many others had to be invalided. Two of the captains were amongst this number, so, in August, I found myself in command of the 'Great Western,' and took her to sea with only a chief officer and one midshipman.

I immediately sent all the white men left of the crew to England, and filled up their places with blacks, after which I had no more yellow fever troubles. The chief officer was first-rate at handling the black gentlemen, and we got on very well, the principal thing being to guard against their sleeping when on the look-out; a negro is like a bird, the moment the sun goes down he wants to go to sleep.

I was left in command of the 'Great Western' till the end of the year, and was then superseded, and ordered to join the 'Thames' as chief-officer or sort of nurse to the captain, who was, more or less, of an invalid.

I returned to England in this ship in March 1853. We had a severe passage, had to put into Fayal for coal and repairs, and it was the twenty-eighth day after leaving St Thomas before we reached Southampton. We remained there a few days, with the pumps going all the time, and then went round to Northfleet Dry Dock for a thorough overhaul, the ship being almost fit for condemnation ; in fact, the consul at Fayal proposed this course whilst we were there, and I believe it would have been the case if I had not opposed it.

I was fortunate at this crisis in having Commander Houston Stewart on board, who gave me his advice and assistance ; the captain being very unwell at the time, everything devolved on me.

I remained attached to the ship till May, and then was sent out to take command of the 'Medway.'

I proceeded as passenger in the 'Magdalena,' of which the old gentleman who commanded the 'Forth' (and before described) was the captain. We left on 17th May, 1853.

As the steam-tender that brought the mails off was about to leave the ship, a gentlemanly-looking man went to the captain and said,—

'I have come down from London in a hurry to take passage in this ship, having just heard of the death of my brother at Panama, and it is necessary I should not lose this mail. I am sorry to say that, in my haste, I left my despatch-box on the seat of my father's carriage, and I have not sufficient money on me to pay my passage.'

The ship being about to start, the captain had not time to go into the matter, and referred the party to the purser, whom he apparently satisfied, as he was allowed to proceed in the ship. He called himself Captain Archibald Logan, King's Dragoon Guards.

It turned out afterwards that he was a private in the regiment, and, moreover, a deserter.

When we arrived at St Thomas the bank would not 'do his bill for him,' so he was handed over to the 'Trent' to be taken to Colon, where he promised to make payment.

When the 'Trent's' boat went ashore at Sta. Marta, he managed to obtain permission to go in it under plea of seeing some friends there; somehow he forgot to return in the boat, and that was the last the 'Trent' saw of him.

Though we had several army officers on board, he managed to deceive all of them, and, wonderful to relate, there was not an army-list in the ship.

I joined the 'Medway' on arrival at St Thomas, and proceeded with her to Jamaica; on the return passage bringing up General Bunbury, who had been in command of the troops.

This was a wonderful old gentleman, and of a tremendous size.

The superintendent at Jamaica, Captain W. S. Cooper, R.N., had knocked two cabins into one to accommodate the general, but had forgotten to have the door made wider; consequently, when the good man arrived at the cabin, he could not get in. The superintendent, who accompanied him down, of course expected to receive some thanks for his kindness, but when the general found he could not pass the doorway, he turned round to the superintendent and abused him royally.

The latter, being a fiery naval officer, was equal to the occasion and gave the general as good as he sent.

The general gave us all a benefit on the way up. I had to rig a house for him on the quarter-deck, and keep two hands off the watch to attend on him. He took some kind of medicine every four hours, and nips of wine or brandy between times, and was constantly sending for the doctor to feel his pulse, as he felt sure he was sinking fast.

He lived to vex the good folks at his club for some time, however, after his arrival in England.

I made a second trip from St Thomas to Jamaica and back, and lost the purser, head-steward and three hands, from yellow fever, in the fortnight.

On the way back a captain of the West India Regiment was ordered to take passage ; he had got into the hands of a money-lender named Arnaboldi, and Mr Arnaboldi told me, even if the captain sold his commission, the proceeds would not pay him more than five shillings in the pound, so he was determined he should not leave the island.

The superintendent sent for me, and said the

captain was to be got away, by hook or by crook, and I was to see to it.

Accordingly, I interviewed the captain and he put himself in my hands. The steamer was to leave at eight o'clock next morning, and was lying at the buoy off the wharf, all ready for sea.

I told the captain to dine at his mess in Spanish Town as usual, and after dinner to drive over to Kingston, and arrive at an appointed place at 10-30 P.M., where he would be met and properly instructed.

Mr Arnaboldi had placed two bailiffs on board the ship to arrest the captain should he embark, and had told me he had taken such precautions that should he (the captain) be able to elude them, he would give him a clean receipt for all he owed him.

I said,—'Mr Arnaboldi, you may as well hand that receipt to me now, for the captain will certainly go away in the steamer, such being the superintendent's orders;' at which he said,—'D—n the superintendent!'

This, of course, put me on my mettle, and I said, —'We shall see.'

When I got on board, I looked round about for one of my crew who somewhat resembled the captain in size and colour of hair, and pitched upon the boiler-maker, and this good man fully entered into the plan.

I arranged with him and three of the engineers

that they should come and ask my leave to go on shore when I was standing near enough to the bailiffs for them to hear what I should say. When they came, towards sun-down, I said, 'Yes, but, Mr Boiler-maker, if you come on board drunk' (the man was a teetotaler) 'I will have you locked up.' 'All right, sir,' said the boiler-maker, and away they went, the engineers in their uniform, and the boiler-maker with his overalls over his uniform.

All remained quiet till just before eleven, when a hail of '"Medway" ahoy!' in a very drunken voice, was heard from the wharf. I was on the look-out for it, and called out, 'There is that drunken boiler-maker again,' and ordered the officer of the watch to send a boat to bring him off. In a short time the boat arrived alongside, with the boiler-maker (that is to say, the captain in the boiler-maker's overalls) seemingly very drunk, in the bottom of it, also the three engineers who had gone ashore with the boiler-maker. These and the boat's crew, with much apparent difficulty, got the drunken man on board, illuminated in their work by the lights the bailiffs had in their hands.

When they had him up, I ordered him to be carried down the engine-room stairs, and locked up in the waste-locker for the night.

This was done, and without the bailiffs having the slightest suspicion that they were helping to get the man on board they were trying to arrest.

As we were about to leave in the morning, the bailiffs came to me and asked permission, as their man had not put in an appearance, to go down in the ship to Port Royal.

I readily assented, at the same time telling them they must find their own conveyance on shore, as I would not land them. They told me the officer of the guard would land them.

When we arrived at Port Royal, I got hold of the officer and told him what had happened, so he refused to land 'the limbs of the law,' as they termed themselves, and they applied to me.

After some little altercation, I agreed to put them on one of the large mooring-buoys in Port Royal Harbour, and they could remain there till a shore-boat came for them. This was accordingly done, and, when our boat was once more hoisted, I backed the steamer close up to the buoy and sent my prize captain up to ask for the receipt their employer had promised, 'For,' said he, 'I am off in this steamer; so tell Mr Arnaboldi good-bye for me,' and away we went. No one but the superintendent and my crew knew that I was mixed up in the cutting out the debtor captain!

CHAPTER VII.

I DID not go back to Jamaica again in the 'Medway,' as I was transferred to the 'Clyde' shortly after, and by the time I did go back, Mr Arnaboldi was dead.

My next command was the 'Clyde,' one of the original Transatlantic steamers altered for inter-colonial service, and I must say it was *so* altered that, as the saying is, even its own mother would not have known it.

I have never seen such an ugly vessel in all my travels. It looked very like a Chinese junk, with paddle-wheels and a black funnel added. A lady who voyaged in her said, 'She is a vile imitation of "La Plata,"' a ship that had been built by the Cunard Company, and sold to the Royal Mail Company after the 'Amazon' was burned.

However, I must not speak ill of the 'Clyde,' as it was whilst I was in command of her that I was married at Demerara, on 24th March, 1854.

I left Demerara with my beautiful young bride on the night of the 25th, and went to St Thomas, calling at all the islands on the way, and, after a few days there, on to Jamaica.

When nearing St Juan, Porto Rico, I found the ship was on fire in the spirit-room, and I did not get it out till after we arrived in the port, when, fortunately, we succeeded.

This fire, I consider, was caused by an incendiary, as the ' Avon ' was fired in the same manner, and at the same time, in the harbour of St Thomas.

At that time the spirit-room in all the ships had gratings at the upper part of the bulkheads for ventilating purposes, and through one of these a lighted candle had, probably, been thrown ; it was hardly possible for a fire to have occurred from any other cause, as the spirit-room was in the square of the hatchway, and had a light through the ship's side, and was only allowed to be opened at 11.30 in the forenoon ; no artificial light was, therefore, required ; besides which, there were always the third officer and the master-at-arms present when it was opened, such being the regulations of the Company.

On arrival at Jamaica, a very searching inquiry was held .by the superintendent, and we were all exonerated from any blame, and I received a handsome testimonial from the passengers, which was the first one I ever had.   At the present time, indeed, I have enough of them to paper a room, besides many others of a more substantial character.

In March 1855 I returned to England, and was again placed in command of the 'Medway,' employed as a horse transport in the Crimean War.

The ship was fitted up at Southampton, under the superintendence of the transport department, and we left early in May, with 221 horses, and the officers, men, etc., belonging to the X Battery of Royal Artillery, under the command of Captain Connell, commonly called in the Service 'Dolly Connell,' a highly-qualified and popular officer.

When we were two days out, we fell in with a May gale. The horses on the upper deck caused the ship to roll badly, nearly the whole of the fittings gave way, and we found ourselves, with the 221 horses, adrift, and the R.A. officers and their men very sea-sick. Our men did the best they could, but Jack does not know much about horses, and the consequence was, the next day we found sixty-seven horses dead and quite as many lamed; several had been thrown from the upper deck down to the lower deck through the skylights.

I took the precaution, as soon as matters were a little squared, to get the officers to meet and draw up a testimonial to myself and the officers of the ship, which they did willingly.

This document served the Company in good stead later on, for no sooner did the R.A. officers recover from their sea-sickness than they began to find fault with the strength of the fittings, and I had to fight our side of the question by telling them the ship had been fitted to carry horses, and not beasts nearly the size of elephants, such as their gun and waggon horses were. Moreover, I contended that the fault was in having all the horses slung, and thus preventing them from helping themselves a little. At that time I did not know anything about horse carrying, and only started this argument in my own defence, but I have since learnt that I was right, and that a horse should only be slung when it shows signs of weariness from standing.

When we arrived at Gibraltar the commanding officer there held an inquiry and surveyed the fittings, which were pronounced insufficiently strong, and were accordingly strengthened by the dockyard artificers.

The complement of horses, after having landed all those lamed, was made up with the largest Spanish mules that could be had, and we proceeded to Balaclava, calling at Malta and Constantinople on the way.

At Constantinople we were given a sailing transport to tow as far as Balaclava. This was my first experience of towing ships—I had plenty of it to do later.   We duly arrived off Balaclava, but it was several days before we were allowed to enter the harbour, as there was no berth in it for us.   We had to keep in sight of the signal-station all day, and at sunset to stand off and lay-to for the night.

During the time we were off the port, there were at least a dozen steamers going through the same manœuvres.

One of the vessels was laden with boots for the troops, and an officer of the commissariat was sent on board, with orders to the master of her (we were not dignified by the name of captain) to carry him down, at once, to Constantinople, land him there, and return.

On the way down this officer told the master of the vessel his errand was for the purpose of picking up all the boots he possibly could, as the troops were very much in need of them.   The master of the vessel said,—

'My ship is full of boots, and I have been trying to get them landed for the last fortnight; let us go back.'

'No, no,' replied the officer, 'my orders are to go to Constantinople, and your orders are to carry me there, and these orders must be carried out.'

So this officer obtained his holiday, and when the

transport returned to Balaclava the soldiers got their boots ; at least we may hope so.

This sort of blunder would not have been made by the French, as all their transports were under the orders of the military authorities.

English transports are always under the orders of the Royal Navy, and it takes a good deal of red tape to get matters fixed up.

For instance, an English transport arriving reports itself to the senior naval officer, who, by-and-by, communicates with the senior military officer, and so on. All this takes time, more particularly as the Royal Navy and the British Army are very like oil and water when brought into contact in a business way.

Why, to this day, when the officer in command of the military wants to send anyone in his department as passenger in a contract-steamer, he is unable to give the order himself, I can't see ; but he cannot. He must apply to the senior naval officer for an order for the officers and men named in the margin to be conveyed in the contract-vessel. I think it is time this sort of nonsense was done away with.'

In due time we got into Balaclava and discharged the X Battery, and then were sent outside again to wait for orders.

Before many days I received orders from the

Royal Mail Company to hand over the command of the 'Medway' to my chief-officer in due form, and to take command of the 'Trent' as soon as we should come across her, for it was reported by the authorities that the captain of the 'Trent' was keeping a kind of liquor-shop on board, so he was to be superseded, or the ship would be discharged from the transport service.

Whether the report was correct or not, I cannot say, but as the 'Trent' was earning 3s. 6d. a minute, and the Government finding coal, the wishes of the Admiralty had to be attended to. Accordingly, when the 'Trent' arrived from Kertch, I went on board, and the captain handed over the charge of her to me.

As he would certainly be discharged by the Company when he got to England, I consider he was a fool for giving up his ship, as there was no power out there that could have compelled him to do so. After I had taken over the 'Trent,' I received orders to proceed to Koslon, coal the ship from the mine there, and proceed to Constantinople for orders.

The engineer informed me, before he could go any further he must have some coal. Accordingly, I went ashore and told Admiral Boxer, who said he had no coal to give me; I must get across as best I could. So back I went on board and explained this to the engineer, but he was not to be put off, and asked me to allow him to go and see the admiral.

He went, and the admiral said to him,—

'You want coal, Mr Engineer, do you?'

'If you please, admiral, I do.'

'Very well,' said the admiral, 'you can go to the devil and rake cinders, that's all the coal you will get out of me.'

When the engineer arrived on board with his discomfiting answer, another difficulty presented itself. I did not know where Koslon was, and had to go on shore to find out. Nobody seemed to know more about it than that it was somewhere on the south shore of the Black Sea. It was not marked on the chart, and that was all the information I could get.

I waited till nightfall, and then left under slow speed and steered across, due south.

At daylight the next morning I had the land in sight, and, by breakfast time, I was well inshore but could see no signs of any coal. I sent the boat ashore, and got information from a Turk, whom we could not understand from his language, but only by his gestures, that Zungledek and Koslon were to the westward.

We therefore started along shore to the westward, and sent the boat ashore at every likely-looking spot. The first time we found a saw-mill running by the water of a small rivulet. The second time we saw coal, and found that place was Zungledek, and that Koslon was still to the west, so we went on, and, at 4 P.M., saw coal on the shore, and sending the boat we found we were at Koslon. Before going in too close, I went in the boat and took soundings, and before dark got the ship to an anchor, and the Government official (English) in charge of the mine came on board and made all arrangements for beginning to coal the ship in the morning.

The process was very slow, as there was nothing in the shape of a lighter, and the boats brought off about half a ton in each, and Johnny Turk handed the coal up in baskets that held about 20 lbs., and made a good fuss about the 'hard work' at that.

The anchorage also was quite unprotected, and I had to go to sea twice on account of the swell coming in.

We were there fourteen days taking in 500 tons, and I got so tired of it that I did not wait to quite fill up, but left for Constantinople, and was ordered to go alongside H.M.S. 'Queen,' and take on board the guns belonging to H.M. Floating Battery 'Meteor,' Captain Beauchamp Seymour (now Lord Alcester), which craft we were to tow to Kinburn, where the allied fleets were occupied in destroying the forts belonging to the Russians.

The 'Meteor' was a craft very much in the shape of a large pie-dish, and we had a rare job to tow it. In the first place it could not be steered with any dependence, and could of itself only steam in and out of harbour, and was thus entirely dependent on the steamer towing it.

I was, therefore, ordered to stand by it, whatever happened.

It had been towed out from England by H.M. ships, and they would appear to have had enough of it.

We started with it early in the morning, and got through the Bosphorus all right early in the afternoon, and, passing by Odessa, which Captain Seymour wished to look at, were fired at by the forts of that place, but fortunately were just outside the range of the guns, and only just, as several shots fell barely short of me.

As I was not paid to be shot at, I sheered off notwithstanding the remonstrance of Captain Seymour.

What object there was in going so close in I could not perceive, as we were not likely to be able to observe anything that was going on ashore, and there was the chance of our getting hit, and, possibly, disabled.

When we arrived at Kinburn, we found the forts had been destroyed the day before, so we were too late, and the next day Admiral Sir Edmund Lyons sent for me and said,—'You brought the "Meteor" here so well that I am going to order you to take her away again and tow her to Kazatch. The sister vessel, the "Glatton," will start at daylight to-morrow morning, in tow of H.M.S. "Valorous," and as I don't wish you to be at sea more than one night, you must go out through the Eastern Channel.'

I remonstrated at this arrangement as the chart showed only twenty-seven feet water in the channel, and my experience of charts had taught me there were sometimes shoal-patches in these shallow channels that had been overlooked in the survey.

However, the admiral was very positive, and so worded my sailing orders that, whatever happened, I was clear.

I was to follow H.M.S. 'Valorous' and 'Glatton,' at all events till we were through the channel, and then I was to make the best of my way.

I had the honour of being included in the dinner-party that evening on board the admiral's ship, 'Royal Albert,' and felt a very small fry amongst so many big fish. It was the admiral's guest-day, but I was taken in hand by the admiral himself, and was seated between him and Captain

Sir Leopold M'Clintock; was taken on board by Lord Alcester in his gig, and introduced to everyone, including the present Admiral Algernon Lyons, who was then flag-lieutenant.

They were all astonished to find me in command of such a ship as the 'Trent,' and still under thirty years of age.

We left the next morning, and I found the 'Glatton' was not a bit more handy to manage than the 'Meteor.' The captain of the 'Glatton' had rigged up some kind of a steering apparatus, in the shape of two spare spars, but it did not answer, and I found the 'Meteor's' plan was the better, viz., to lash her rudder amidships and remain passively astern of her tower.

As soon as we got out into ten fathoms water, I put all my power on, and very soon passed the 'Valorous,' and lost sight of her and the 'Glatton' astern, before dark.

I succeeded in getting the 'Meteor' into Kazatch the next afternoon, but the 'Glatton' did not arrive till well into the next day.

We were employed several days getting the guns and stores from our ship into the 'Meteor.' The guns were sixty-eight pounders, and pretty heavy to lift out of our hold and swing over to the 'Meteor,' alongside of which we were moored.

At last, however, all was accomplished, and I

was ordered to proceed to Constantinople, and
thence to Malta, where we received orders to go to
Barcelona, and load mules, etc.

Having got out of the way of having bills of
health, I forgot to take one before leaving; and,
on arrival at Barcelona, we were placed under
observation for thirteen days.

We were anchored in the quarantine ground,
and all hands had to go ashore at 11 A.M to be
examined daily by the health-officer.   This examination consisted of our all being arranged
along one side of an iron railing in line, and the
officer walked down on the other side, and, as he
came, each one had to put his tongue out for him
to see.

No time was lost over this farce, as the mules
were not ready, even when we were released.

At length they arrived, 260 in number, and
were taken on board, with a large quantity of
forage, also 200 Spanish muleteers.

These were a very cut-throat-looking set of
rascals, and we concluded they were brigands of
whom the country was glad to be rid.   They gave
a good deal of trouble on the voyage, as they did
not approve of the Government rations, which was
the only food we had for them, and were not used
to rum, but demanded wine, of which we had none
to give.

I was obliged to put into Malta to get these points settled, which did not take the admiral long to do.

We also received orders there to land them all at the Dardanelles, instead of going on to Balaclava.

After having landed the mules, etc., I proceeded to Constantinople. I may here state that I landed the mules into the charge of Oscar Marescaux, who at that time was the paymaster of the Land Transport Corps, and whom I met afterwards in the West Indies, attached to the Colonial Bank. At the time I am now writing, he is the manager of the Jamaica branch of that bank, and goes by the name of King Oscar; he has always been a good friend to me.

At Constantinople I had an amusing scrimmage with H.B.M. Consul, Cumberbatch by name. This gentleman wanted to treat the transports as British merchant ships, and required them to take out a Firman each time they passed through the Bosphorus; this we did not see, as it did not matter to us whether we went through the Bosphorus or not; it would appear to be the affair of H.M. Government.

I accordingly made a report on the subject to Admiral Grey, and handed him the copy of the extract of the 'British Merchant Shipping Act' requiring all ships under the British merchant flag to deposit their register and articles of agreement with the consul (if any) at the foreign port of call. As I considered the 'Trent' was a passenger-ship for the time being, and exempt from these regulations, I had not hitherto paid any attention to the Act. On this occasion Mr Cumberbatch gave me notice that, if I did not deposit my papers within the twenty-four hours following, he would put the law into force.

The admiral, considering I was right, decided to help me out, so appointed Commander Thomas Brewer, R.N., to join the 'Trent' as agent of transport, which changed the British merchant red ensign into the agent's blue ensign and pennon.

The next morning, as I had not conformed to his orders, the consul sent his son on board with a Posse Comitatus of Dragomen, etc.

I received the young gentleman very graciously, and when he and his party arrived on the quarter-deck, he ordered the crew to be mustered, and proceeded to read the extract of the Act which I was considered to have broken.

When he arrived at the words—'All vessels under the British merchant flag,' I stopped him and told him his father had sent him on a 'fool's errand,' for the 'Trent' was not under the British merchant

flag, as he would see if he only lifted his eyes. He
looked up, and for the first time noticed the blue
ensign ; at the same time the agent came on deck,
and in the proper naval language of the day inquired what the devil was up, and ordered Mr
Vice-Consul out of the ship, at the same time
desiring me to get the ship under way, and he
would give me orders where to go.

I can fancy old Cumberbatch's dismay when he
found himself outwitted by a common merchant-
sailor, which he told me I was, when I last interviewed him.

We proceeded, under orders, to act as senior
officer in the Dardanelles, to see all transports
made the best of their way through, as supplies
were falling short at Balaclava ; sailing-vessels we
were to tow through, as the wind generally was
blowing down the channel and a strong counter
current running.

Our usual station was Bashi Ka Bay, a few miles
below the entrance of the strait.

As our old agent (he must have been well on
towards eighty years of age) was much afflicted
with rheumatics, etc., I had to watch for what
I called his lucid intervals, and then get him
to sign blank order memorandum papers that
were wanted to give orders to steamers going
through, to tow a sailing ship as they went, so as

(to use the agent's language) 'to save Her Majesty's coal.'

On one occasion one of the Royal Mail Company's steamers came along with Sardinian soldiers on board ; we brought him to, and sent him an order to tow a collier called the ' Abeona ' through. As this was the only one wanting a tow at the time, it was not worth while for us to get steam up.

When the captain saw the order was in my handwriting, although signed by the agent, he said he was not going to take orders from a junior officer (he was one place higher on the list than I), and I had considerable trouble to make him believe I had an agent on board, as I could not produce him, the old gentleman at the time being in bed, and his head protected from draughts by a band-box ; however, he thought better of it through the night, and in the morning relieved us of the ' Abeona.'

We remained performing this duty for some weeks, when we received intelligence of H.M.S. ' Apollo ' having gone ashore, in a snowstorm, on the north side of the Sea of Marmora.

The agent ordered me to proceed to her assistance, so we started off in search of her. We shortly found her aground, with only eleven feet of water around her, on a sandy bottom, with her head to seaward. She had taken the ground whilst going about; and as it happened at the top of high water, and at the time of the highest tide, there was no hope of moving her without lightening.

This we proceeded to do, trying, occasionally, to tow her off at high water, and so carried on till I had everything out of her and on board of the 'Trent.'

This had all to be done in the boats of the two ships, and took a month.

Before commencing to lighten, I laid her two bower anchors out ahead of her, with a hundred fathoms cable on each, and when everything was out I anchored the 'Trent' seventy-five fathoms farther out than the anchors of the 'Apollo,' and backed in till I had a hundred fathoms of cable out.

We next passed an eighteen-inch cable from the 'Trent,' and when all was ready and nearly the highest tide on, I made another attempt and succeeded in hauling the 'Apollo' ahead eleven feet, but she would not come off.

We still had one more day to expect more water at high tide, but I did not want to lose another fortnight, so we filled some oil cans with gunpowder, and with some brass tubing out of our ship managed to explode them just under the 'Apollo's' bows, and heave and tow at the same time.

I had the satisfaction then of seeing the ship move the moment of the explosion, and she came off, and that so fast I had to do all I knew to prevent her running into my stern, as the wind was off shore.

Having got her off to her anchor, the next trouble was to keep her from capsizing. I hauled her alongside of me and shot her ballast (which I had lying on my main deck) into her as fast as possible, and worked on getting her tanks on board all night, filling them with salt-water, pumped in by my ship's fire-pump.

By morning we had her safe; rested my crew and the 'Apollo's through the day, and left with her in tow at nightfall for Constantinople.

CHAPTER VIII.

IN the previously-recounted history of the 'Apollo,' I have forgotten to say the commander of that ship shot himself as soon as the ship struck, and as his executive-officer was the same man who had been officer of the watch when the Royal Mail steamer 'Actæon' was lost, and a second master in the navy, my agent was, of course, his senior officer, hence I took charge of the business, for I did not think much of Mr Second Master, who, I found, had abandoned the 'Apollo' and landed all the crew on the beach the morning after the ship struck, without having made the slightest attempt to save the vessel.

We found them living on shore under canvas when we arrived, and embarked them all on board the 'Trent.' There never could have been any danger, as the ship was not a hundred feet from the shore, and I thought we had very good proof of this, for, when the men came off to the 'Trent,' the ship's corporal brought his canary on board with him, using his lantern for a cage.

We had considerable difficulty in towing the 'Apollo' when we got into narrow waters, as her rudder had got unshipped and was on board my ship, with its pintles bent, or I would have shipped it before I started ; however, my experience with H.M.S. 'Meteor' stood me good service, and I got her to an anchor off Scutari.   The next morning, without accident, I handed her over to the captain of H.M.S. 'Queen,' the flagship.

We received a very complimentary letter from the Admiralty for getting the 'Apollo' off, and what was more to the purpose, £300 were awarded us, to be shared out acording to the monthly pay of each of us, and the letter ended with the words— 'for praiseworthy exertions, fortunately crowned with success.'

We were next ordered to Balaclava, there to receive orders from Admiral Freemantle, who had succeeded Admiral Boxer.

We anchored outside as we had nothing to land, and the next morning the 'Queen of the South' arrived.   This was a large, auxiliary screw-steamer, heavily rigged as a barque.   The wind was blowing right into Balaclava Harbour, and the ship was given too much way, which the captain discovered too late to be able to get off by going full speed astern, and she charged into a tier of small Greek vessels lying at the port side of the entrance.

As the 'Queen of the South' passed under our stern, I saw she had too much way on, and called out to the captain, who appeared strange to the place, to go astern all he could; but the wind acting on the vessel's yards, the engines not being of sufficient power to overcome the way, three of the Greek vessels were sunk.

The captain had noticed the engines did not seem to be taking the way off the ship, and thought that, although the order for going astern full speed had been given, it was not being obeyed, so he kept calling out, 'Go astern, will you; go astern! Do you call this d—d thing a steamboat? Go astern, I say!' All the time dancing on the bridge in a most frantic manner. Suddenly it struck me I had seen this sort of arrangement going on before, and I recognised in the captain of the 'Queen of the South' one of the old Royal Mail commanders who had retired four years before, Sharp by name.

As he had always been the one in the service who handled his ship best, I had some difficulty in making out how he had made such a blunder on this occasion.

The explanation of it was that, hitherto, the

steamers he had commanded were of the full-power paddle-wheel type, and would go astern as well as they would go ahead, and also go back to where they came from, whereas the 'Queen of the South' was a screw of small power, and required very different handling.

Captain Sharp was one of the oldest steam commanders, and had gained his experience in the steamers running between London and Leith.

He had the honour of bringing H.M. Queen Victoria from Leith, in the ship under his command, in the early part of her reign, and there was a good story about it, told by himself.

The old gentleman always began his tale by saying,—'You see, ladies and gentlemen, when the Queen came on board, I was considerably flabbergasted, and not knowing better, I went up to her with my cap in my hand, and said, "How de do, marm; glad to see you on board, marm," and held out my hand to shake hands with her. I saw all the fine people about her looked astonished, but could not understand why, but at same time their looks made me feel uncomfortable. However, Her Majesty (as I have since learnt to call her), like a good, kind soul as she is, saw my difficulty, and, putting out her hand (which I took hold of, instead of kissing as I was told afterwards I should have done, and shook) said, "I am very glad to get on board, Captain Sharp, and I am told you will take me safely back to London if anyone can." I said, "I will; you may depend on it, marm," at which she laughed, and down below she went.

'No sooner was she gone than a naval captain, with his sword and his three-cornered-scraper gold hat on, comes up to me, and "Captain," says he, "do you know what you've been and done?" "No," says I, ' what is it?" "Why," says he, " you have insulted the Queen, calling her 'marm' and shaking her hand like an ordinary woman!" Says I, " People don't often laugh when they feel insulted, and the Queen she laughed as she went away, anyhow; so" I says, "you can tell that yarn about the insulting to the marines, for I, as a blue-jacket, arn't going to believe you." "Well," he says, "we won't argue the point; get your ship under way at once."

'So off I went, and we got started with H.M.S. "Black Eagle" in company. By-and-by, when we got outside, up came the Queen on to the bridge, with a beautiful purple velvet gown on. The naval captain came up too; he still had his sword on, but had doffed his scraper-hat.

'The Queen called him Lord Adolphus Fitz-clarence when she spoke to him, and asked him all sorts of questions as to what place this was, etc., but soon found he did not know anything about it, so she tackled me instead, and I then found she talked not like an *ordinary* woman, but like a very *extra*ordinary woman. She wanted to know about everything, and laughed at a good many things I told her. She did not say anything about my having insulted her, and soon made me feel quite as much at home with her as I generally did with any other lady - passenger on board.

'When the Queen came up from dinner, she inquired of me how many knots we were going? I told her nine. She turned to Lord Adolphus (who stood, generally, about three feet behind her), and said,—" My lord, signal to the men-of-war, and ask how many knots they are going." By-and-by, he came up and said,—" If you please, your Majesty, they answer eleven."

'The Queen turned to me, and said,—" How is it, Captain Sharp, you tell me this steamer is going nine knots, and the men-of-war say they are going eleven, and we are beating them?" "You see, your Majesty," says I, "what they're a-going by is the passengers' log." "Passengers' log, Captain Sharp; what is the meaning of the passengers' log?" "Well, I'll tell your Majesty," says I. "You know, I once drove an opposition coach." "You drove a coach, Captain Sharp; I should not have liked to have been inside it." "Well, please your Majesty," says I, "not exactly a coach, you know, but an opposition steamboat, and we always put two knots extra into the log to please the passengers, who will always go in the fastest ship. That's how we call it the passengers' log."

'This seemed to please the Queen mightily, and she laughed like a big school-gal, and so, too, did Lord Adolphus.

'Next day the weather began to get bad, and all the Queen's lady attendants got sea-sick, and the Queen kept below a good deal looking after them. Towards evening I made up my mind we were going to have a dirty night, so I proposed to Lord Adolphus to put into Lowestoft, but he did not want to, so I watched till the Queen came up, and I went up to her and told her we were going to have a very dirty night. She said,— "Well, Captain Sharp, what do you propose to do?" "Well, your Majesty," says I, "I thought of putting into Lowestoft, but that there naval lord of yours says no." "Never you mind him," says the Queen, "I came on board for you to take care of me, and you had better do it;" so I sings out, "Hard a-port" to the man at the wheel, and on to the bridge I goes.

'We got comfortably into Lowestoft, and lay

there for the night, and it did blow, by jingo! Before the Queen went to bed, she came up and sent for me, and when I got alongside of her, she says,—"You did right, you did, Captain Sharp! and I am much obliged to you."

'We got under way again the next morning quite early, so as to get out before any of the shore folks knew the Queen was about, or we should have had the mayor off with one piece of paper, and some other fellow with another piece of paper—they calls them addresses; and the Queen said she had had plenty of these sort of things in Scotland, and did not want any more just then.

'We got safely up to Gravesend, and before the Queen would land, she sent for me to the gangway, and said,—"I am very much obliged to you, Captain Sharp, for bringing me along safely and comfortably: and is there anything I can do for you?"   "Well, your Majesty," says I, "if you like to make me a lieutenant in your navy, I should be glad."   "I am afraid," said the Queen, "I can't do that.   It would require an order in council."   "Well, your Majesty," says I, "I thought it would not take you long to give it, but I don't want to give you any trouble.   I will be contented if you will only give me the purple velvet dress you had on when you came on

board, and I will always wear a cap made of
a piece of it."

'She did not appear to think this unreasonable,
and promised the dress should be sent. She
could not give it me then, as it was packed up.
In due course the dress came, and here is my
cap made of it.   God bless the Queen!'

The orders I received from Admiral Freemantle
were to repair to Kazatch and place myself under
the orders of Captain Beauchamp Seymour, and to
tow H.M.S. 'Meteor' from Kazatch to Spithead.

Before I left Admiral Freemantle, he made me
promise that I would stand by the 'Meteor' till I
anchored her at Spithead.

When I arrived at Kazatch, I went on board the
'Meteor' and reported myself, and returned on
board my own ship, where I found an officer from
H.M.S. 'Leopard' inquiring why I had not been on
board that ship to report myself to the senior officer.

I told him I did not know anything about senior
officers ; my orders were to report myself to Captain
Beauchamp Seymour, and I had done so ; anything
by way of report to the senior officer I always had
understood should go from him ; at all events, I
was not going on board any more ships to make
reports.   I would show him the sailing orders, if he
liked, or he could take them on board with him to

the senior officer, as they were run out now I had arrived at Kazatch and seen Captain Seymour, who would give me his orders from time to time, as directed by Admiral Freemantle.

I did not hear any more of the senior officer, except that Captain Seymour told me I had got him into hot water with the captain of the 'Leopard,' but he did not seem to mind it much.

The next morning I hauled alongside the 'Meteor' and commenced taking the guns and heavy stores out of her, and in about a week left with her in tow for Spithead.

We had a hard northerly gale when about half-way across the Black Sea, and I was obliged to round to for twenty-four hours, as I was afraid to run for the Bosphorus in bad weather, knowing the difficulty of steering the 'Meteor' with the wind aft, and I was also chary of getting down on a lee-shore with her behind me.

Shortly, however, the weather moderated, and I got her safely through the Bosphorus and anchored off Scutari.

The experience I had gained in this gale was of great service to me during the remainder of the passage, as I had to round to for bad weather several times before I got her home.

At Scutari it was found the 'Meteor's' rudder had got defective in the gale, and it had to be

unshipped and sent ashore to the Turkish dockyard to be repaired.   This occupied several days,
during which I had a good opportunity of visiting
Constantinople and the places round about.   At
the time we were there was the Feast of the
Ramadan, and I saw the Sultan moving about in
his state caique most days, but, of course, a dog
of an infidel like myself was not allowed very
near.

I don't know a finer sight anywhere than the
Mosque of St Sophia soon after sunrise on a fine
morning, with the Bosphorus studded with caiques
with the occupants in their festal attire, and the
boats belonging to the foreign vessels pulling
about in order to see the Sultan's procession on the
way to the mosque.

It is impossible to exaggerate the beauty of the
Bosphorus and the Golden Horn, and it is quite
impossible to give anything like an adequate
description of it.   I should advise folks to go and
see it themselves, and to choose the time of year
when strawberries are in season, if they have a
weakness for that fruit.

I have never found in any part of the world
such strawberries as I got in the market at Stam-
boul.

When the rudder was repaired we left for
Malta, and got on all right till we were close to the

island, where it came on to blow a hard easterly gale, and we were frightened to take the harbour with the 'Meteor' behind us, as we could do very little by way of steering her with the wind aft, so we passed round the south end of the island and hove to, under the lee of it in quite smooth water, for two days, after which we got safely into Valetta Harbour.

Here it was found the apparatus for condensing fresh water for the 'Meteor's' crew had gone wrong, so we were in for another week's delay. This I did not mind, as it was still early in the season to tow such a machine as the 'Meteor' across the Bay of Biscay; but the stay at Malta was irksome, as there is nothing much to be seen and we had very little to do on board after we were coaled up.

At Malta, however, on this occasion, an amusing incident occurred. One of the crew was an old man-of-war's man; he gloried in the name of Jemmy Harper. If ever there was a thorough reprobate, Jemmy was one, but a smarter sailor there never was; aloft he was like a monkey; he seemed to fly about the rigging without taking hold of anything.

He never missed a chance of getting drunk. Once being in a man-of-war, the captain of which went by the name of Paddy Quinn, Harper was mustered amongst the 'liberty men,' when the captain said to him,—

'Now, Harper, if you come back drunk, I will order you three dozen.'

'Beg your pardon, sir,' said Harper; 'you may as well serve out half of them at once, as I shall most certainly get drunk, if I swing for it!'

At Malta, Jemmy came to ask leave to go on shore, and got it with the understanding that he would not get drunk; of course I knew full well he would.

When he returned, drunk as usual, he was locked up till he should get sober.

When he was brought up next day, I said to him,—

'You know, Harper, you promised me you would not get drunk, and yet you did.'

'Well, sir,' said he, 'I believe you would have got drunk yourself under the same circumstances.'

'You mean,' said I, 'if I had put the same quantity of liquor inside of me?'

'I don't mean anything of the kind,' said he; 'and if you only give me a chance, I'll tell you.' 'You know,' he continued, 'very well, I have a wife at Southampton; well, when I was out here, in H.M.S. 'Galatea,' I got married again, and for some years have been bothered with two wives. Yesterday, when I got ashore, I found my Maltese

wife had died a few days back and left a few odds
and ends, which I sold, and also a bit of money in
the old teapot. I was so glad to find I could no
longer be brought up for having two wives that I
sat down and had a good drink; and I believe, as
I said before, you would have done the same.'

What could be done with such a man as that?

We next got as far as Gibraltar and had more
work with the condenser, but Captain Gray, R.N.,
drove us out in a very short time. Now, as far as I
could make out, the officers of the 'Meteor' had
made up their minds to be present at a grand ball
that was to come off on the next Thursday—as we
left on the Tuesday—and did not relish the idea of
being sent to sea!

We had only got as far out as Tarifa Point when
the signal was made on board the 'Meteor,'—'Bear
up for Gibraltar, port hawse pipe has given way,
slack port tow rope and tow by starboard one.'

The method of towing this unwieldy craft was
by two eighteen inch cables (hemp), the Elliot eyes
of which were shackled on to the 'Meteor's' bower-
cables, so they could not chafe through in the hawse,
When we got round, I noticed the 'Meteor's' port
cable, instead of being passed out of the bower
hawse pipe, had been passed out of the warping
hawse pipe, and the strain had carried it away and
part of the bulwark round the bow.

I saw no reason for going back on this account, and suggested stopping and unshackling the towing hawser, and passing the chain out, as usual, through the bower hawse pipe. However, I only got snubbed for the suggestion, and the signal went up—'Obey orders.'

When we got back there was a grand hullabaloo and a court of inquiry as to who was to blame, with the usual result of these inquiries—that no one was.

That it had been done on purpose I did not doubt, as, had both cables been passed out of the bower pipes, it would have taken too long to get an anchor ready when we arrived at Spithead.

Of course the repairs were not finished till after Thursday, and all my engineers and the boiler-maker were paid for working at it, as well as the ' Meteor's,' so that no time should be lost.

This was the last delay of the voyage. We started with two new twenty-four inch hemp cables for tow ropes, and except having to heave-to twice for bad weather, had no mishap, arriving safely at Spithead in fifty-four days from Kazatch.

We averaged 144 miles per day, which was considered quite a feat for a vessel like the ' Trent.' The ' Glatton ' was towed home by one of the Cunard steamers in thirty-seven days, but they did not make such long stays in harbour as we did.

I had received orders from Captain Seymour to anchor him a cable's length from the Spit buoy, and to do that had to pass through the two lines of the North Sea fleet lying at anchor at Spithead.

Although I had shortened in the tow ropes to fifty fathoms, instead of a hundred, the 'Meteor' still sheered very much, and as we passed each ship the lower booms were topped up for fear the 'Meteor' would strike them, and as I came to the 'Duke of Wellington,' the admiral's ship, old Charlie Napier sung out from his stern gallery,—

'Anchor sir, anchor sir; you will be foul of the whole fleet!'

'No fear,' replied I ; 'I towed her twice through the Black Sea fleet, and did not touch one of them.'

The 'Meteor' had the signal to anchor flying, but I knew Captain Seymour did not wish it, so I went on till we arrived a cable's-length from the Spit buoy, when I stopped, and the 'Meteor' was able to anchor.

Notwithstanding my disobedience to orders in not anchoring, I was commended by the port-admiral for having brought the 'Meteor' in safely, Captain Seymour having sent in a favourable report.

I made two more trips to Balaclava, each time

bringing home a battery of artillery, which were no longer wanted before Sebastopol, as peace was declared.

Before leaving the Crimea, I witnessed the review of the Allied Armies, which was a splendid sight. I had been present at the attack on the Malakoff and Redan, had seen the Battle of Tchernaya, and was in Sebastopol on the Thursday, as it was evacuated on the Tuesday, and saw all the horrors of the hospitals in the dock-yard, and after all was over I saw the Naval Review at Spithead by H.M. Queen Victoria in August, 1856 ; on the review-day I was one of the Royal Mail commanders sent on board to assist the commander of the 'Atrato,' and as the 'Atrato' was the fastest ship present, we had a good time, and followed H.M. yacht as closely as we were allowed.

Before closing this part of my narrative I will here insert a detailed account of the loss of R.M.S. 'Tweed.'

A TRUE ACCOUNT OF THE WRECK OF THE ROYAL MAIL STEAMER 'TWEED,' BY A SURVIVOR.

'The R.M.S. "Tweed" left Havana for Vera Cruz the 9th February, 1847, in the evening, with sixty passengers, and a crew, including officers, of ninety-two. The weather was fine, with a light, variable wind, which settled to southward, with a fresh breeze which lasted sixteen hours; the weather becoming thick, attended with vivid lightning. At midnight of the 10th the wind shifted suddenly to north, and blew a fresh gale; weather still thick, with no possibility of getting any observations.—11th, the gale still continued, with same thick weather. At noon (11th) the latitude, by account 22° 32' N., and longitude 87° 32' W., give the bearing a distance of Alicran shoal S. 86°, W. 120 miles. The course was shaped W.S.W. The fore-sail, fore topmast stay-sail, fore and main try-sails being set at 3.30 A.M. of 12th, the look-out forward sang out "breakers ahead." The captain (who was on deck) ordered the helm to be put hard a-starboard. The engines stopped and reversed (the ship being, by the reckoning, at least thirty miles to southward of Alicrans). With the way, however, she had on her, and the sail that was set, she forged ahead, and struck, though only lightly at first. The second time she struck so violently that the cylinder of one engine was forced upwards a considerable distance, and both were entirely disabled. The engineers were obliged to abandon the engine-room. It was now evident that the ship would become a complete wreck. I had made the best of my way on deck when she struck the second time, and was holding on, together with a number of half-naked passengers, to one of the starboard funnel-stays, hoping, with my companions, that the ship would hold together till daylight. To ease her as much as possible, the masts were ordered to be cut away; the ship striking so heavily it was with difficulty we retained our hold. The starboard boats were stove by the sea into a thousand pieces. The ship at this time gave a heavy lurch. The funnel went over the side, together with the three masts. She now heeled over to starboard with deck to seaward, thus allowing the sea to make a complete breach right into her. The upper works parted from her bottom; a piercing shriek was heard from the unfortunate women and passengers who had not succeeded in reaching the spar-deck. We now were holding on to the port-side (that is, the few that were enabled to reach there). Some of the crew and passengers lowered the gig and port-cutter, but they were so fearfully overloaded that they swamped as soon as they touched the water, and only a few regained the deck by the falls. At this moment a heavy sea broke over the ship, and striking the bell seemed to toll the knell for the death of those who perished in the boats. The ship was now fast breaking up; a heavy sea took away a great part of the stern as though it had been cut off with an axe. I was holding on by one of the cutter's davits, and with a few others was of opinion that the port paddle-box held out the greatest chance of safety. With the captain among our number, we endeavoured to gain it, but scarcely had gone half-way when the ship parted amidships, and I was washed overboard; the return sea brought me back again, and the captain gave me his hand and assisted me to reach the rail, to which I clung.

'I was soon washed off again, and recollect nothing till I found myself close to the captain on the main-mast (or some other large spar).

'I was again washed off, and again pulled on by the captain. A sea then struck him with such violence that I thought he would have been dashed to pieces by the shock.

'This separated us, and I did not expect to see him more. The next wave carried me away, I know not where, but I have an indistinct recollection of being washed to and fro amidst broken pieces of timber, and finding myself, half stupefied, seated upon a floating piece of wreck, with several others. This proved to be the stern-post, with the after sky-light and part of the spar deck. Here we held on, expecting to be washed off with every roller. We even took leave of each other, so little did we expect to survive our unfortunate shipmates.

'In the midst of our danger our fears were lessened by seeing smooth waters inside the reef, which assumed the appearance of land, and, whilst calculating our chances of escape, our raft touched the bottom, and we were comparatively in smooth waters.

'Dark as it was, we could see the paddle-box —the only remains of that once magnificent ship, the labour of many months.

'We heard voices on what we supposed to be the shore, and, having scrambled through the wreck, found ourselves on a reef, together with about twenty-five others, amongst whom was the commander, covered with blood and much injured. Here, half-naked, shivering with cold, and not knowing where we were, we sat down, and, having offered up a prayer to Him who had thus relieved us, awaited with anxiety the break of day, still entertaining the hope that the dark appearance around us was the land, and that those whom we left clinging to the paddle-box were still in safety, and that at daylight we should be able to render them some assistance. Never was dawn of day more anxiously looked for, and never did it appear longer arriving. At length it came, but only to show us that we were surrounded by the wide ocean, without the slightest appearance of land. We then looked at the paddle-box, where were

still clinging many of our shipmates, the sea
running completely over them, and a heavy surf
breaking in upon the reef, so that we were unable
to render them the slightest assistance. We next
commenced a survey of our own condition. We
found that the driest part of the shoal upon which
we were was only six inches above water, and
about two hundred yards inside the reef, it being
at this time low-water, and though we were assured by the captain and officers that the rise
of the tide could not exceed three feet, we
could not but be afraid they might be mis-
taken. Looking at the dark side of the picture,
our imaginations portrayed to us a lingering
death, and we almost envied those whose troubles
in this world were past. Still, however, buoyed
up by our hopes, we exerted ourselves to the utmost of our ability.

'Three of the boats were found inside the reef—
namely, the mail boat, one lifeboat and one cutter.
These were immediately examined. The cutter
and lifeboat were so much damaged as to be
utterly useless. The mail-boat's stern was torn out
of her, and she was otherwise much injured ; but,
as there was a possibility of making her serviceable,
the captain determined to try, intending, if successful, to send her to the Campeachy coast for assistance.

'Some of our number, accordingly, set to work, collected some nails from pieces of the wreck, and, with a copper bolt for a hammer, tacked some pieces of tarpaulin and canvas round her bows, and on to various other parts of her. Others commenced forming a raft, on the shoal, of the masts and spars, whilst a third party collected such provisions as were washed our way.

'All this time we were obliged to look on and see the number of those who were holding on to the wreck gradually decrease, although the slightest aid in the world would have saved them; but, alas! it was not in our power to give that aid. Some we saw go down close to the wreck, some midway; whilst others reached the shore so exhausted that the return sea took them back, and we saw them no more. Only a very few, who would have shared the same fate, we were enabled to save by means of an oar or a boat-hook.

'The second officer came on shore about an hour after daybreak, naked and much cut. He could not swim, but stripped off the few things he had on, jumped overboard, and fortunately reached a beam, on which he came ashore.

'By 5 P.M. the boat was finished, though she was far from sea-worthy, and a raft of about thirty feet square and four feet high was formed, on which were two casks of flour, a small keg of oatmeal, a cask of vinegar, one of butter, a small keg of brandy, three or four cases of wine, two hams, a side of bacon, three pigs—two of them alive—a live sheep, and sundry other things, but not a drop of water!

The tide had now risen three feet, and was still flowing. The captain now ordered all to muster on the raft. In number we were seventy-six—seventy-six having either met with a watery grave, or still were clinging to the wreck. One of the passengers had saved his Bible and Prayer - book (bound in one). He was solicited to read prayers, which he did with great solemnity, and one and all joined in the responses. This finished, the captain ordered the chief officer (Mr E. Ellison) to go in the boat, accompanied by seven of the crew. The American consul for Vera Cruz was asked to go as Spanish interpreter, and Lieutenant Davis, the Admiralty agent, went by his own request. Some oatmeal, a few bottles of wine, a compass (that had providentially been washed on shore uninjured); a sufficient number of oars that had been picked up, also a boat's mizzen leg and mast were put into the boat. Instructions having been given to the chief officer to steer due south for the coast of Campeachy (a distance of nearly 160 miles), there to report our situation, and, if possible, to bring us assistance, we gave them three cheers as they sheered off, and watched them out of sight, not without a foreboding that we had taken leave of them for ever.

'It was now getting dusk; the wind had in some measure subsided, and the surf was less high. Not having tasted any food the whole day, we mxed some oatmeal and butter, moistened it with a little wine, and served out a ball, about the size of a small apple, to each; the crew being served first, then the passengers, the officers receiving their share last. After this the neck of a bottle filled with wine (scarcely half a glass) was served out in the same order, and our repast was finished, and thankful we were for it, frugal as it may appear.

'Being overcome with our exertions, wet and cold as we were, we lay down, and covering ourselves with the wet clothes we had picked up, slept soundly for some hours. In the middle of the night a cry was raised that the raft was moving; we got up and found it was a false alarm. The depth of water was taken, and found to have increased very slightly, so we lay down and again fell asleep. Before daylight we were all up, and, as soon as there was sufficient light, prayers were again read. About a thimbleful of brandy was then served out to each person, and we were divided into parties for various purposes, everyone as orderly and obedient as when the

unfortunate ship ploughed the ocean.   Our first
thought was of our poor companions, and, looking
at the paddle-box, we saw, to our horror, their
number had fearfully diminished.   We could count
only seven!   A few of us were immediately sent to
the nearest point, to see if any assistance could be
rendered them, but alas! the breakers were still
rolling in so heavily on the reef it was impossible.
We shouted to them, and by signs endeavoured to
persuade them to make an attempt to reach the
shore, for, by remaining longer exposed to the heat
by day, and the cold by night, without food, we
well knew their strength would soon be utterly
exhausted.   They took our advice, but out of the
seven only three succeeded; the rest perished,
making in all seventy-three souls.   We now commenced work.   One party was sent along the reef
to look for provisions, another to collect timber
to enlarge the raft, and a third to carry stones to
form a breakwater round it, each party being under
the command of an officer.   Those who were too
much injured to do such hard work remained on the
raft, spread out the wet things to dry, stowed the
provisions in the snuggest possible manner, and
made everything on the raft as comfortable as
circumstances would permit.

'About eight o'clock (as near as we could
judge by the altitude of the sun) we all re-

turned to the raft with such things as we had been fortunate enough to pick up, and received a small cake of flour and butter, a piece of raw ham, and the neck of the bottle full of wine ; but before the wine was served out, as some were complaining of thirst, the top of a smelling-bottle (that had been picked up), full of vinegar, was given to each.   For this we were very thankful, as it allayed greatly our feeling of thirst. We then resumed our labour, for we had to take advantage of the early part of the day before the tide became too high, as the walking about up to our middles in water was very laborious, and our physical strength was in some measure decreasing.

'It is a remarkable, and, at the same time, a most providential circumstance that, out of the whole number saved (though there was not one altogether uninjured), there was only one seriously hurt. This was a passenger for Mexico, having his wife and child on board ; and, when the first alarm was given, he rushed aft to the ladies' cabin to endeavour to secure them. He had been there but a few minutes when his wife was washed away from his arms, then his child—both of whom perished. He himself was carried away with the stern of the ship (as mentioned in the preceding part of this account), and reached the reef with the loss of three fingers of the right hand. The ragged ends were cut off with a penknife by the surgeon, and dressed as well as circumstances would admit. He bore his sufferings with manly fortitude.

'During this day (13th), as we passed along the reef, we saw many bodies, both of passengers and crew — some dreadfully mutilated, showing that their deaths must have been occasioned by great violence, during the breaking up of the vessel. Others were not so, and had, in all probability, been drowned from inability to swim. Our provisions, also, were increased by seven bottles of wine and a piece of pork; several other articles were picked up, amongst which were two or three papers of candles and a box of lucifer matches. These we considered a Godsend, but, unfortunately, they were wet and would not ignite. We exposed them to the sun and tried again, but with no better success, so we put them safely away to try again on the morrow.

'We now took our second and last meal for the day, which was similar to the morning, heard prayers read, and, sitting down, talked upon the two subjects that engrossed our thoughts — the probable safety of the boat, and of ourselves. We then lay down and slept, suffering greatly from cold and wet.

'In the morning (of the 14th) we were up, as

usual, before daylight, and, when it arrived we
scanned the horizon with more anxiety than we
had hitherto done as the feeling of thirst was becoming prevalent, and there appeared but little
hope of relieving it. We looked at the heavens
and speculated on the chances of rain, and viewed
every heavy-looking cloud with a feeling of hopeful
anxiety. We now had recourse to pieces of linen
steeped in vinegar to moisten our mouths, each
then had the neck of the bottle filled with brandy
served out to him, and, after a few prayers, we
commenced our day's work—the greater part being
set to carry stones to the breakwater, while the
remainder went to look after provisions. The sun
this morning burst out with more intensity than
on the previous days, and our matches were again
exposed to his rays. In a short time one was
tried, and a hearty cheer, which could not be sup-
pressed, broke from all present as it ignited. A
candle was lighted, and this we looked upon as
the most fortunate occurrence of the whole. Our
hopes were raised, our energies redoubled. We
now speculated boldly on the time we could exist
in our present situation should anything happen to
the boat, and succour from that quarter be cut off.
Various calculations were made and schemes devised.
In short, we viewed it as a merciful interposition of
Providence, and everyone's spirits were elevated.

'No time was lost in preparing a place and materials for making a fire—one corner of the raft was appropriated for it; some sheets of iron were stripped off the wreck, upon which were laid some of the driest pieces of wood, and a fire soon blazed forth. The dead sheep were skinned and cut up, some fish we had caught were cooked; we made some cakes with flour, butter and wine, and, for the first time since we left the ship, we had a hearty meal. But care was taken not to serve out too much, for our number was large, and our stock of provisions very small. Moreover, we knew that, the more we ate the more we should suffer from thirst. After this we had the top of the bottle twice filled with claret, and after resting a little resumed our work. As we found there were plenty of fish to be caught (both cray fish and rock cod) our anxiety with regard to food was considerably relieved. It was the want of water we dreaded, for though up to this time we had suffered but little inconvenience from it, we feared the consequences of spirituous drink for any length of time. We therefore endeavoured to construct an apparatus for distilling salt water. A leaden and a copper pipe having been picked up, the engineers contrived to bend them, and fitted, as well as they could, one into a jar, the other into a tin can, and we commenced our distillation; but in consequence

NIGH ON SIXTY YEARS AT SEA.   153

of the imperfection of the apparatus, the process
was exceedingly slow, and though it was carried on
all day, not more than two bottles of water passed,
and this was so much impregnated with salts of
lead and copper that we were afraid to drink it;
so we had to reclean the pipes and commence
again. During the day, three more bottles of wine
were picked up, and as our stock received no
further addition, we also got the main-mast and
two or three other large spars, and made them fast
to the raft, which now (being surrounded by a good
barrier of stones) assumed an appearance of some
little strength; but when we looked around and
saw the sponson and wheel (which still held on in
their former position), with a small bit of the ship's
side that lay on the reef, and considered that it
was all remaining of that mighty vessel, made
strong by art (under every advantage) to resist the
fury of the tempests, and remembered that in one
short half-hour the waves had dashed her to atoms;
and when we, too, beheld the surf at so short a
distance, rolling in upon the reef, it made us
shudder, I say (when we looked at our small
raft, put together in a hurry), to think how entirely
we were at the mercy of the elements. But still
we trusted and prayed that He, who had snatched
us from an untimely end and extended to us so
many mercies, would not desert us now.

'(15th.) We were up to view the grey dawn of morning, and beheld the breaking of the fourth day on the wide waters. Some had been up all night distilling water, and had succeeded in making a bottle and a half, which was free from the deleterious properties of the first distillation. This was so small a quantity amongst so many, that we corked it up and put it by to administer to the greatest sufferers, or till sufficient was obtained to serve out to all.

'After prayers each had a small quantity of brandy, mixed with vinegar, served out to him. The captain deemed it prudent to commence a floating raft, as we now had the large spars for a framework, and sufficient rope for lashings, and, moreover, it was next to useless to send parties along the reef to look for provisions, as nothing now remained of the wreck. So our working hands set about it, and by mid-day a good substantial framework was completed, which, when planked over and finished, would have carried us, provisions and all, though we should not have resorted to it till the very last extremity. Our boat had been gone now nearly four days, and every hour increased our anxiety and our fears for her safety. We thought of her feeble condition when she started, the probability of her being carried out of her course by currents, of her not

being able to get clear of the reefs, in the first
instance, and, even should she succeed in reaching
the coast, of her getting to a part of it where no
assistance could be obtained. In fact we dis-
cussed, as we had done every morning previously,
all the mishaps that could possibly befall her, and
we came to the same conclusion (for our hopes
would admit of no other), viz., "That she was safe,
had arrived, and would send us assistance in the
shortest possible time." .This, miraculous to relate,
proved true; for, as we were resting ourselves
after our exertions at the raft, a cry was raised—
"A sail! a sail!" Every eye was turned to the
spot. It was but a speck on the horizon, and
various were the opinions respecting it. Some said
it was a rock they had seen in that direction before. But, as it became more distinct, everyone
pronounced it a sail. Then its character—Was it a
fishing boat, a schooner, a brig, or a ship? Then
its destination—Could it be for us? No!

'The time was too short; it was a fisherman
going to Perez, a vessel passing by only. Then,
would she see us? On these points our fears were
soon allayed, our hopes gratified. A fine little brig
was distinctly made out standing towards us, and
as she neared and we saw a large boat, with a
mast in it, towing astern, not a particle of doubt
remained as to her mission. By four o'clock she was

abreast of us, hove-to about a mile and a half outside the reef. The large boat she had towing
astern, and a small one he lowered, were pulling
towards us! We were saved! No expression of
joy escaped us; our feelings overpowered us, but
we fell on our knees and returned thanks to
Almighty God for thus especially taking us
under His protection. The two boats were
now alongside our raft, and in one of them
was our chief officer, on whom we showered our
congratulations for his safe return, and our thanks
for his conduct. His tale was soon told. He was
compelled, the first night, to make fast to a rock,
and cleared the reefs the following morning and
made the best of his way to the coast. On the
morning of the 14th he fell in with the Spanish brig
"Emilio," about five miles off Sisal, having been
blown out of the roads in a norther. He and his
boat's crew were immediately taken into Sisal, some
provisions and water put into the brig, a large
canoe was hired, and her captain, without any loss
of time, came to our rescue. We immediately put
as many passengers into the two boats as they
could with safety convey through the surf, and as
the evening was now closing in, the rest of us remained patiently on the raft till the morning. The
canoe remained with the brig, the small boat returned to us, and in her was the captain of the brig,

who resolved to stay with us on the raft for the night (his mate being a man in whom he could place the utmost reliance), in order to allay in our minds any fear of the vessel leaving in the night.

'As soon as day broke, we had prayers and looked around for the brig, but she was nowhere to be seen, nor did she make her appearance till the afternoon, the current having swept her away further than any calculation which had been made. This only shows how dangerous the currents must be at this season of the year. By 3 P.M. the canoe was alongside of us, and another load got into her, as also into the small boat; but the day was by no means so propitious as the preceeding; the wind had increased and the surf with it and though the canoe succeeded in getting through the surf, the small boat capsized; no one was drowned, but all were too much frightened to risk it again. The brig, being likewise dead to windward of the reef, was obliged to keep at a much greater distance off than would have been necessary in finer weather. A consultation was therefore held, and it was determined that we should all embark in the two boats and go to Perez, a small, uninhabited island to the southward of the reef, and the brig was sent round there to pick us up. These arrangements being made, we began our embarkation as quickly as possible, the evening beginning to close in. The captain was the last man to leave the raft, and himself cast off the boat's painter. We reached Perez about 1 P.M. on the following day, after spending a more trying night than any of those on the raft; nor was it unattended with danger (so much so, that we were obliged to anchor), on account of the difficulty of distinguishing the channel between the shoals. The canoe was so crammed that we could not alter our position for the whole night; the dew wetted us through like rain, and our teeth chattered with cold. But as we knew our trials were nearly ended, we bore it without a murmur. As the brig was not in sight when we arrived, we landed. It is a small island, with a few huts on it, in which the fishermen live when they come there in the season to catch turtle; there is plenty of water, which is brought by them in casks. We lighted a fire by the aid of our matches, cooked some ham, and made an excellent meal.

'The brig hove in sight just as we had finished. We went off to her, half at a time, and were all on board by 5 P.M., and off for Sisal, where the captain of the brig was obliged to go first, as he was loading for Havana, and had come to our assistance without the knowledge of his owners, who resided at Merida, the capital of

Yucatan. We reached Sisal the following morning, where we were received by the inhabitants with the greatest kindness, and never before, I should imagine, did such a motley group set foot in the clean, quiet little town. Everyone strove his utmost to relieve our necessities and administer to our comfort, and much did we require it, for we were crippled to a man, and now the excitement was in some measure over, we began to feel our infirmities the more.

'As we were to go to Havana in the same brig, we had to remain at Sisal some days, till she was ready, receiving all the time the greatest kindness from everyone. We embarked on February 25th for Havana, where we arrived on 3d March, and remained there till the arrival of the R.M.S. "Avon," in which we took our passage for England.'

PART II.

CHAPTER I.

I CONSIDER the Crimean War marks the great turning point in ocean steam navigation, and shows, in a very bright light, the wisdom of the British Government in establishing the Contract Packet Services which had commenced running during the fourteen years preceding the breaking out of the war. They alone were able to put their hands on large steamships, fully officered and manned, and to equip them for transporting troops in a marvellously short space of time, by taking advantage of the private dockyards of the large companies who owned the vessels. They were also able to assist the French Government in transporting their troops, and, if I recollect rightly, all the Sardinian troops were transported in these English contract vessels.

As soon as the war was over, foreign governments commenced subsidising steam-lines, and the result has been that, ever since, competition has arisen and a wonderful improvement, both in the size and speed of mail and passenger steamers has taken place.

When the British Government first contracted with the Royal Mail Steam Packet Company in 1839, the ships were to be of 1800 tons and the average speed seven knots; between 1839 and 1850 this speed was raised to nine knots, and a class of larger vessels became necessary; but still the steamers could only carry sufficient coal to take them across, and anything of consequence in the way of cargo was out of the question.

The contract packets were simply mail and passenger steamers, and as such they remained for some years after.

The French Government, however, soon began to turn its attention to the Contract Packet Service, and now the English steamers have to contend with considerable opposition from French steamers (heavily subsidised) on most of the lines, of which previously they had enjoyed the monopoly.

But it remained for the enterprise of John Elder to completely revolutionise steam navigation by inventing the compound marine engine, in or about the year A.D. 1860, and enabling steamers to run at a higher speed with a very reduced consumption of coal.

It took some time before the Royal Mail Company adopted these engines, as they never have been fond of trying experiments; the Admiralty holding them very strictly to the terms of the contract, they wisely allowed outsiders to try the value of new inventions.

It was not till 1870 that the 'Elbe,' the first vessel with John Elder's engine fitted in it, came into the R.M.S. Company's service. This ship was very troublesome for some voyages; she had the defect of not being able to start when required, through some complication in the slide valve of the high-pressure cylinder. She was not the only vessel which was thus troubled, for on one occasion when starting from St Thomas and the fit came on the 'Elbe,' one of John Elder's engineers happened to be in the harbour, in charge of the Compagnie Generale's steamship 'Martinique,' and, when he heard of the 'Elbe's' difficulty, went on board of her to find out about it, advisedly on account of his firm.

This gentleman was profuse in protest against the slide valve being allowed to get jammed, and said 'such a thing had never happened with any other ship, and that there must be some neglect somewhere.' Whilst he was expatiating, a message came to him from the 'Martinique,' requiring him to return on board at once, as they had tried to move the engines preparatory to starting, and the high-pressure slide valve had got jammed. So away he went, with his tail between his legs, as the saying is.

Nevertheless, the compound engines of John Elder soon gained favour, and were used everywhere till a new era set in, when they all got put aside by the triple expansion-engine, which apparently will run on for some time.

CHAPTER II.

I WAS now appointed to the 'Thames,' and sailed in September, 1856, for St Thomas, to take up the Intercolonial Service.

The 'Thames' was the first ship to leave Southampton for the West Indies in 1842, and was then considered a first-class steamer, but now the mighty had fallen, and she had to take a back seat.

I commanded her till the end of 1857, and then was moved into a more modern vessel—the 'Solent,' a flightier-looking ship than the 'Thames,' but not nearly so serviceable, or so comfortable for either passengers or crew, though a trifle faster.

I was relieved from her early in 1858 and went home as passenger in the 'Parana,' and on arrival was placed in command of the 'Teviot,' another of the old originals.

This vessel was chartered by the European and Australian Company to run the mails and passengers from Southampton to Alexandria, whence they were transported across the isthmus to Suez in four-horse waggonettes.

This was a pleasant service, and the passengers we carried were very amusing folk, particularly those coming home from Australia, many of whom were the descendants of those original settlers who took their passage out at the expense of the British Government, and had not been provided with a passage back again.

The first voyage I had the Mayor of Melbourne on board, who was sent home to deliver the contributions from that city to the Patriotic Fund.

This gentleman (?) expected to have been knighted by Her Majesty, but somehow he wasn't, and had to find his way back to Melbourne rather quicker than he intended, by advice from Scotland Yard.

As soon as he came on board, he watched me out of my cabin and then went in and left his card.

I returned the compliment by sending one of my pasteboards to his cabin by the bedroom steward.

Mr Mayor's object, I was told, was to get a seat close to me, but as he had no lady with him, I was not inclined to allow him to carry it out.

There was another character on board—a lawyer from Sydney—and this gentleman had a young family with him.   He had arranged with the agent at Sydney that he was to be supplied with four quarts of pure milk daily, and had taken the precaution to have words noted on his ticket to that effect, which, he explained to me, implied a contract.

As we had only one cow on board, and over one hundred passengers, this milk contract was rather a staggerer, more particularly as our individual cow occasionally took upon herself to stop the supply of milk, as far as she was concerned, altogether, and neither the Milk-Maid brand, or any other of preserved milk was in vogue at that time.

There was no help for it but to take on board a couple of goats and make the best of it.   Mr Lawyer was not satisfied with this arrangement, and said his children required pure cow's milk, and that was what his contract contemplated.

I suggested the contract merely said *pure* milk, and did not state cow's milk or any particular milk, and that I should consider the contract was fulfilled if I could only give him four quarts of pigeon's milk, provided it was pure ; however, the cow and the two goats were not equal to the occasion, and when I got to Malta I sold the goats and bought two cows, as I was not anxious to give Mr Lawyer a case to amuse him in England at the Royal Mail Company's expense.

The Company did not lose anything by it, as they deducted the cost of the milk from the Sydney agent's commission, which I hope taught him not to make foolish contracts with passengers by way of currying favour with them.

There was also another amusing incident. A few days after leaving Alexandria there was turtle-soup for dinner, the prospect of eating which seemed to delight an old gentleman, who was travelling under the charge of his wife, a much younger person.

The good lady sat opposite to her husband, who in due course was served with his soup. He was allowed to get it fixed up to his taste, but as he was about to start consuming it, madam reached across the table and snatched his plate away, leaving the poor old man with the spoon in his hand. 'You *sha'n't*'! she said. Moral—be careful how you get married to a young wife when you are old; I wouldn't.

I was much troubled at the very dowdy appearance of the passengers, and was obliged to fall back on the Company's regulation, 'That passengers were to appear at table respectably dressed;' but as the amount of respectability was not specified, I was rather at a loss. However, after thinking the matter over, I remembered the advertisement usually in the corner of the *Times* :—

'Wanted—Ladies' and gentlemen's cast-off wearing apparel, for Australia.'

This I cut out and pasted on the main-mast early one morning.

After breakfast, when the passengers were moving around, I went up to the advertisement and began reading it, which, of course, brought several others to read also. To these good folks I said,—

'I have often seen this advertisement, but, till now, I had been unable to discover the object of it, and I am sorry to find that Australians really do dress themselves in other people's left-off clothing.

I had no reason to complain after that; there was a large demand for trunks from the baggage-room, and at dinner that day there was much 'purple and fine linen' displayed and an excess of jewellery; one successful digger's wife had on a handsome black silk dress, and no less than seven gold brooches ornamenting the front of it.

It was very amusing to notice the jealousy between the Sydney people and the Melbourne people. The one set had very little to do with the other, and there not being a smoking-room in the ship, where they would probably have got thrown together, I had two distinct parties on board all the way; there was no difficulty in knowing to which set each person belonged, as there was a marked difference between them. Sydney people were good old-fashioned people, whereas the Melbourne folks were of the latest date, which I did not consider an advantage.

Fortunately, however, they did not quarrel, although each party looked down on the other.

This service did not last long, and by the end of the next year I found myself off to the West Indies with the ship, to take up Intercolonial Service again. We went out without either passengers or mails, so had nothing to amuse us but the study of nature.

One afternoon we passed close to a very large drifting spar and soon after saw a larger one, which I thought was worth picking up; we accordingly stopped, lowered a boat, and towed it alongside; it took a great deal of trouble and some time to get it hoisted, and when we got it up it was found to be valueless, as the side that had been under water was eaten through and through by the teredo. We obtained several fine specimens of this troublesome denizen of tropical waters, which was all the return for our labour, and then let the spar go adrift, possibly to gull some other gullible folk like ourselves.

We were now getting into that part of the Atlantic where hurricanes were to be met with at this time of year, and a good look-out on the barometer had to be kept, and other warnings, showing the approach of these dreadful storms, looked for.

I consider the hurricane season proper commences with the full moon in August, and does not end till the full moon in October, and that the third day after the first quarter of the moon is the most dangerous time of the month, but, of course, as I have only been navigating in these waters forty-eight years, I can't be supposed to know much about it !

As the ship had very little in her, I took the precaution to have the yards sent down on deck and the topmasts housed by the time we entered the Tropics. I also had the boats all taken on board and lashed. The weather continued fine, and there was no appearance of any change.

About two days before we were arriving at St Thomas, I found the ship's barometer falling, and although my aneroid kept working steadily and the water continued smooth, I felt somewhat anxious, and watched the sky constantly till we got into St Thomas Harbour.

I found everyone there in a contented state of mind, and on inquiry found the barometers were standing at their usual height, whilst mine had fallen steadily and was down to 29.4, or over half an inch lower than other people's. I could not make this out, till someone suggested perhaps the mercury cistern was leaking.

On examining it, I found this to be the case. The barometer was a very old-fashioned one, and had a leathern bag to contain the mercury, which had worn thin, and was allowing the mercury to filter through. Had I used my brains, I should have saved myself a good deal of uneasiness.

This taught me to place more confidence in my aneroid, which at that time had not been long invented, and was not generally in use for sea purposes.

CHAPTER III.

AT St Thomas I received the mails and passengers for Mexico and Havana, *ex* the 'Magdalena,' as the 'Teviot' was to go on the Gulf of Mexico route.

Amongst the passengers was a small girl about eight or nine years old. She was handed over to me with a label tied round her neck, on which was written 'Whilimena Bodmin, passenger to Vera Cruz. To remain on board the ship till fetched.'

It appears the child had been put on board the 'Magdalena' at Southampton and there left with a few clothes tied up in a large cotton handkerchief, and labelled as she was when handed over to me.

On the way out the lady passengers had taken pity on the child, and formed a Dorcas club, with the result that, instead of her small bundle of clothes, she had a box full of garments that no young lady need have been ashamed of. The captain of the 'Magdalena' had allowed the carpenter to make the box, so she arrived with a first-rate outfit.

As no notice had been sent to her parents, who were up at the mines near the city of Mexico, the child was not fetched on our first arrival at Vera Cruz, and I had to take her on to Tampico with us, and await the chance of her being claimed on our return.

Fortunately her parents received the letter announcing her arrival in time to get down to meet the ship on her way back again; otherwise, the poor thing might have been taken back to St Thomas, and obliged to make a second trip to Vera Cruz.

People seem to have perfect faith in the Royal Mail steamers, and send their children along with no other protectors than the captain and stewardess.

On one occasion, when in command of a Transatlantic ship, a very pretty coloured girl, about thirteen years of age, was brought from Demerara in the 'Arno,' and transferred to my ship, the 'Tagus.' I was to take care of her, as usual. She was the daughter of a Wesleyan minister at Demerara, and I must say one of the best brought up children I have had to do with, and did not give the slightest trouble to anyone. A few days before arrival at Southampton, I inquired if any one was to meet her? She said, 'I don't know.' 'Where are you going?' I asked. She said 'Clapham.' 'Whereabouts in Clapham are you going as Clapham is a big place?' Her answer again was, 'I don't know.'

We arrived at Southampton early on a Friday morning, and, when all the other passengers had been landed, also the specie, my work for the time was over, and I was going home.

There being no appearance of any one coming to meet this child and take her away, there was nothing else to be done but take her to my house, which I did. When I arrived at the door, my dear wife came out to meet me, and, seeing the child in the carriage with me, said, 'Who is she? Where's she come from? To whom does she belong?' It then dawned on my mind that the wife, knowing the manners and customs of the natives of the West Indies, jumped at the conclusion that the child was mine, and that I had brought it home for her to take care of. However, she soon became reassured, and the young lady was admitted, but I saw I had given my dear wife a scare, unwittingly. We made nothing out of this girl till Saturday, when our children came home from school. They soon elicited from her that she had a letter in her trunk, which she had been told to give to me before we arrived at Plymouth; this, childlike, she had forgotten—hence the trouble. On the Monday morning I took the key of her trunk down with me, and sure enough there was a letter right on the top, addressed to the Wesleyan Mission in Bishopgate Street. I telegraphed to them, and they sent for the child that afternoon. This, however, taught me a lesson, for it might have been within the range of possibility that this young lady should have been left on my hands for some months.

On another occasion, a child of six years old was sent up from Antigua. Her parents were both dead, and she was to be forwarded to her grand-parents in Bristol. Going back to my experience, I declined to accept the charge, and returned her to Antigua, incurring the displeasure of the local newspaper by the act, which, however, did not trouble me at all.

The child was sent up to St Thomas by the next mail and handed over to the care of Commodore Revett, who, being less wary than I, took the child to Southampton, where she remained on Mrs Revett's hands for nearly six weeks.

At Vera Cruz I found a large quantity of specie waiting for shipment, which took two days to take on board; it amounted to two million seven hundred thousand dollars, and weighed a hundred and thirty tons, or thereabouts, and I had considerable difficulty to get it stowed away securely; in fact, I put a lot of it in the side coal-bunkers, which proved a very foolish thing to have done, as, before I arrived at St Thomas, the weight had pushed the iron rest of the bunker through the top of the boiler, and we had to· start getting it out on the way, and stow it on the main deck in the open, necessitating an officer's watch over it. On arrival at St Thomas we found the 'Paramatta,' the Royal Mail Company's new ship, had been lost on the Anegada Reef. This ship was the first of a new batch of ships which the Company had built to run with 'Atrato' and 'La Plata' on what was termed 'the accelerated service.' Asthe 'Paramatta' was the ship that should have taken the mail home, it was necesssary to replace her, and the 'Teviot' was appointed for the duty. We therefore took in the passengers and mails, etc., brought up from the islands and the Spanish Main, and started homewards. The specie from the 'Thames,' which had arrived from the Spanish Main ports, amounted to five hundred and seventy thousand dollars, thus bringing up the amount I already had on board to close on three and a half million dollars, which, I believe, was the largest sum ever transported across the Atlantic in any one ship. We had several passengers on board, and left St Thomas very deeply laden, and, as far as I was concerned, with a heavy heart, as I did not see my way to making the passengers comfortable. However, we got on very well, and I landed them all in good humour at Southampton on fourteenth day, having been favoured with fine weather all the way. The only trouble I had was with the baths in the morning; we had but two for gentlemen and one for ladies, and, of course, every one wanted the bath at the same time. I got over the difficulty by hanging up two empty flour barrels, perforated with half-inch holes, on the after end of the bridge, and rigged a canvas screen round them. I superintended this impromtu bathing place myself, and had by far the most of the patronage, as my shower-bath arrangement did not occupy half the time the main-deck ones did, added to which the younger men thought it quite a joke to patronise the skipper's establishment. There was also no time taken up in emptying the bath.

When we arrived off the Lizard, I sent notice of our arrival on shore to Falmouth by a pilot-cutter. I conveyed the message to him in a bottle, and tied a bottle of rum on to the piece of board as well as the bottle containing the message, much to the delight of the crew of the cutter.

After landing the passengers at Southampton,

we set to work to get the treasure landed, and a
grand job we had; there were no steam-winches
fitted at that time in the Royal Mail steamers, and
it all had to be hoisted by hand. There being very
little weight in the ship, she laid down on her beam
ends as soon as the labourers got on to the upper
deck, so we had to send them ashore and lead
the whips on to the quay to do the hoisting there.
At length all was on shore, and stowed in the
railway waggons, and my officers and I started
with it for the Bank of England. At Nine Elms
we had to transfer it from the railway waggons to
Pickford's vans; this took us till six o'clock in the
morning, and we were all pretty well tired out,
having been kept going for two nights and a
day, between coming up channel and the specie.
About seven, having had a bit of breakfast brought
into the station from a coffee-shop outside, we
started for the bank, a string of eighteen Pickford
four-horsed waggons, which took up considerable
room on the road. I had with me, as escort, my
five officers, boatswain, carpenter, master-at-arms,
and three quarter-masters, the sailmaker of the
Southampton yard and his mate, and sufficient
others to place one man inside each waggon,
whilst the superintendent's secretary and I rode up
and down the line of waggons in a hansom cab,
challenging the guard in each waggon now and

again. We made quite a formidable show in the city, but fortunately so early in the morning there was not much traffic. We arrived at the bank—that is to say, the leading waggon did—before the gates were open, and had to wait. I had a good deal of trouble given me by the police, and, of course, was ordered to move on, which it was impossible to do; even when the gate did open, there was not room in the yard for more than a third of the waggons, and the rest had still to remain outside. By the time I had delivered the specie, it was 3 P.M., and by way of receipt I had in my hand a summons to appear before the Lord Mayor at 11 o'clock next day, on a charge of obstructing the streets and non-compliance with the orders of the police. The superintendent who handed me the summons said, 'he had a good mind to lock me up instead of summonsing me;' to which I replied, 'nothing would give me greater pleasure than to have such comfortable lodging for the night, as not only should I not have to pay for it, but I should be able to draw a handsome sum from the city for having used it.' The next morning I duly appeared before the Lord Mayor, and four other city magnates; after the charge had been read, his lordship said,—

'Well, young man, what have you got to say for yourself?'

'I've nothing to say at all, my Lord Mayor,' said
I, 'the business speaks for itself, and your inspector
of police must have been a fool to fancy that I
could move eighteen waggons of silver—of *silver*
my Lord Mayor; mark that, my lord! When
I was learning my duty as an officer, it was always
impressed on me that I should never give an
order without there was a reasonable chance of
its being carried out, hence I deduce that your
superintendent is a fool; don't you think so yourself, my lord, and when I tell you that he talked of
locking me up over the business, I should think
that your lordship would decide that he is a
fool.'

'Well, sir,' said his lordship, 'I shall not be too
hard on you this time, but you must understand,
on a future occasion, that the orders of the police
must be obeyed. I shall fine you 2s. 6d. and 10s.
costs.'

'I am much obliged to you, my lord,' said I, 'but
I think you, at all events, ought not to find fault
with me for a so-called obstruction of the streets,
seeing that the streets were made for the conduct of
public business, and not for anyone's particular
pleasure; my obstruction was for the public
benefit, but last November, I think it was, on ninth
day thereof, I wanted to get along this way, and
the police would not allow me, and on inquiring

the why and the wherefore, I was told it was on account of the Lord Mayor's show. Now, in my humble opinion, it is much more allowable to block up part of the street with waggons of silver, when one has brought the said silver from foreign parts, for the benefit of the inhabitants of this great city, than entirely to block up the streets with a show, which, although the Lord Mayor's, only benefits a few, and gives a grand chance for organ-grinders and pickpockets.'

'Officer,' said his lordship, 'remove that young man from the place. If he stays here much longer with his long tongue, I shall be obliged to commit him for contempt of court.'

'Good-bye, my lord,' said I. 'Think of me when you are riding in the after-carriage of the show on the 9th of November next.'

And I expect he did!

CHAPTER IV.

WE did not remain long in England. So soon as our turn came round for the dry dock, we were put in to examine the copper-sheathing, and that being found all right, were hauled out next tide got ready for sea, and despatched for the West Indies again as soon as possible.

On arrival out, I was transferred to my old ship, the 'Solent.' She had been to England since I left her, and had new boilers, besides being generally refitted and turned into a nice ship. I made my first trip in her along the islands, and formed the acquaintance of Sir Benjamin and Lady Pine, who were going to St Kitts; Sir Benjamin being the governor of that island at the time. I, also, had on board thirteen young women, sent out by the Moravian Mission as wives for the missionaries stationed along the route. None of these young women knew which man they were to marry. Thirteen missionaries had simply written home for wives, and the Society sent out thirteen young women educated for the purpose, each one supposed to be as good as the other!

We arrived at St Kitts at 3 A.M., and the two missionaries, who had sent for wives thence, came off. I had the thirteen young women mustered up in a line, and one missionary said, 'I will have this one,' the other also took his choice, and both went off ashore with their new partners! The remaining eleven went down to bed again; whether pleased or disappointed I cannot say. At Antigua, the same afternoon, three were wanted, and three selected as before, but the Antigua men had a better chance, as they had their view of the young women by daylight. The same process went on at each island as we passed, leaving me only two, after Barbadoes, to go on to Demerara. If I had been in the market, I would quite as soon have had one of the twain that were left, and the last, as any of them.

This must appear to most young women to be an extraordinary way of being fixed up with a husband, but it has always appeared to me to answer very well.

There is a story told of a missionary in Nicaragua sending along for his third wife, and requesting the Society not to send him another red-haired one, as he had already had two with red hair, and the climate did not seem to suit them, they provided him with a one-eyed woman for a change!

I did not remain very long in the 'Solent.' Early in 1860 I was relieved by Captain Montague Leeds, and went home, in command of the 'Parana,' to take the command of the 'Magdalena,' which ship was fitting out at Southampton to run on the Brazil line.

I first sailed in the 'Magdalena' on 9th March 1860 for Lisbon, St Vincent, Cape Verde, Pernambuco, Bahia and Rio de Janeiro. This was a new experience for me, as hitherto my service had mostly been in the West Indies. I did not get on very well at first, as the people did not like me, and I did not like them. I had never been used to such dirty people, and it took me some time, and a good deal of scolding, before I could get them into anything like tune.

It also took considerable space in the local newspapers to publish the abuse lavished on me. However, I stuck to it, and before I left the line I was reputed to be as much of an angel as I had been reckoned a devil to commence with.

Early in my coming on the line, I took out H.R.H. the Duc de Nemours and his son, Comte d'Eu, who was to marry the Princess Imperial of Brazil. On arrival at Rio de Janeiro, I had the honour of being introduced to His Majesty, Pedro II., the Emperor, and Her Majesty the Empress. I found out that the Empress was very fond of rhubarb tart, so whenever I was in Rio I had a large one made on board, and sent to the palace; in return I received, on the morning of sailing, a large cake with the Brazilian arms and colours on it. H.R.H. the Comte d'Eu also presented me with a black pearl scarf-pin when he was leaving the ship.

These honours seemed to cause a turn of tide in my favour and I grew more popular. After the marriage, the Comte and Comtesse d'Eu visited Europe and took their passage in the 'Magdalena' all the way to Southampton. Having landed them safely, I was a made man in the opinion of the Brazilians, and was no longer abused in the newspapers.

Two years after I had taken up the Brazil line, or nearly so, the Slidell and Mason business took place, and the 'Magdalena' was engaged to carry troops to Halifax. On 21st December 1861 I left Southampton for Halifax with the second battalion of 16th Regiment, a company of Royal Engineers and a battery of Artillery, altogether 1400 officers and men and some horses—eleven, in fact. It was first intended that these men should be landed at River de Loup, and I was ordered to go there. The 'Parana,' which sailed on 17th, was also ordered there.

As I had been in the Quebec trade, I knew

there was no chance of being able to get to River de Loup certainly after Christmas. I represented it to the officer in charge of the Transport Department at Southampton, and he got our destination changed to Halifax.

The embarkation took place on the afternoon of 21st December, and by the Transport Regulations the ship should not have sailed till twenty-four hours after. The agent of transports we had on board was anxious to get the ship out of dock before dark, so it was arranged we should go out into the river and wait the arrival of the rear-guard, who were to be sent down in the tender.

The officers of the rear-guard, including the adjutant and the quarter-master, who had remained behind to give over the quarters at Aldershot, finding the ship had gone out of dock and concluding the ship would not sail that night, quietly went to the hotel, purposing to go on board on the morrow.

When the tender came alongside, a letter was handed to the agent on board, which contained an order from the captain-agent of transports on shore, that the ship was to sail forthwith, which we accordingly did, passing the Needles at 10.30 P.M., 21st December, 1861.

When we were clear outside, the chief officer going his rounds discovered that twenty-five court-martial prisoners, who had been marched on board at 3 P.M., were confined in the bullion-room, which had been converted into the prison, and was calculated to hold only nine men.

As this bullion-room had been constructed on the strong-room principle, ventilation had not been taken into consideration, and it was doubtful what we should find when the door was opened. Fortunately the men were all alive, but not one of them had a rag on, and some of them would soon have succumbed from the pestilential atmosphere of the place; in fact, we were very nearly having a second edition of the Black Hole of Calcutta.

The next morning we began to feel the loss of the adjutant and quarter-master; an acting adjutant was soon appointed, as a regiment without an adjutant is very like a ship without a rudder, but the quarter-master was not so easily replaced. Fortunately we had the quarter-master sergeant to fall back on, but this poor man was very much frightened at the responsibility. As he said, 'I sha'n't get any good out of it, and I may lose a lot; I don't like it.'

We started with a fine fair wind and carried it right across to the Bank of Newfoundland. We did not come across a single vessel, but nevertheless the passage was not a monotonous one.

The soldiers caused endless amusement; they were not only Irish, but very Irish, too.

One of the captains had an Irish servant, and this good fellow, by way of facilitating matters and making his master comfortable, sent all the captain's clothes with his wife, and brought along madame's clothes instead; consequently, the first morning out, the poor man had no change of garments, and we concluded madame was in the same predicament.

As soon as this got wind amongst the other officers, plenty of chaff began to fly about. One man, by way of consolation, called out, 'I wonder if Madame X. will ever let you wear the pants any more, Ximmy? It always struck us,' said he, 'she was rather anxious to wear them,' etc. Another asked, 'Can you lend me'—(naming another article of ladies' under-apparel which it would not be correct to mention more particularly).

The colonel was a cracked-pot at the best of times, and the loss of his two staff officers did not add to his stability.

He had a great weakness for court-martials, and one was held every morning at eleven o'clock, on, and around, the after-capstan. Of course, the prisoners were generally found guilty, and usually sentenced to stoppage of grog; fortunately for them there was no room for pack-drill, or they would have had plenty of it.

As my master-at-arms had the serving out of the grog nominally, overlooked by the officer of the day, a plan for working round the stoppage was soon devised.

The grog was served out by the roll-call, that is to say, each man came as his name was called, with his pannikin in his hand. The man under stoppage had his name called also, but came without his pannikin. When the next man came, the master-at-arms put two rations into his pannikin, instead of one. The man then drank only half of the contents of the pannikin and carried the rest away to give to the man whose ration was supposed to be stopped. It was only a day or two before we arrived that this dodge was discovered.

It was amusing to watch the issue of winter clothes to the soldiers. The second day out (the first was Sunday) the sea-kit was served out. This consisted of a duck frock and trousers, which each soldier, as he got it, put on over his ordinary clothing.

Towards the end of the week, warm clothing was issued. This was put on next to the ordinary clothing, and the duck frock and trousers went on again over that, and the usual soldier's great-coat over all.

But the great sight of all was when the winter suit was issued,. consisting of sheepskin coat and trousers, also a fur cap instead of the forage caps.

The soldiers now appeared something like the Arctic explorers at the Royal Naval Exhibition, and looked an enormous size, having so many suits of clothes on, one over the other.

I also found it difficult to know my crew from the soldiers, as each of them managed to get hold of a sheepskin suit and fur cap by some means or other. We had nothing to do with it, as we merely handed over the bales of clothing to the quarter-master sergeant and got receipts for them ; the military looked out for the issuing.

I fear the regiment had to pay a long bill one way and another, but, to make use of a scriptural simile, what was that among so many?

The night before we arrived at Halifax, and when we were close to the Cape Race land, a heavy N.W. gale and snowstorm came on, and continued through the night.

At that season of the year, as navigation was supposed to be closed, all the lights were put out, or rather not lighted, so there was no hope of being able to see any. We could not tell anything of the temperature by the thermometer, as the mercury had gone out of sight, but we felt it was intensely cold, as the ship was one mass of ice from stem to

stern, the sea freezing as it broke over us.   Soundings we were unable to take, as the line froze hard
as it came out of the water, and the men's hands
got frozen and cut hauling it in.

Fortunately the wind was off the land, and the
water comparatively smooth, so we stopped the
engines, and, like St Paul, let the ship drive.

There must have been a strong current setting to
the westward, as, when day broke and the weather
cleared, I steered in due north, and at ten o'clock
made Beaver Island Lighthouse.

We hauled away to the westward, and by 3 P.M.
were well over towards the entrance to Halifax, and
then it recommenced to snow, and I had to stop,
my heart failing at the idea of having to pass
another night like the last.

Whilst I was in the height of my despair, one
of the many seeming miracles that have from time
to time been performed in my favour came to pass.
Close to me appeared, through the thick of the
snow, a schooner of about 150 tons, and as she
passed I hailed and inquired the bearing of
Halifax, and asked if they could send a pilot.   The
captain said nothing about the bearing of the port,
but replied,—

'I will give you a pilot if you will send a boat
for him.'

We started to lower a boat, which was hanging

at the quarter, by Clifford's lowering apparatus. We always kept water in each of the boats to preserve them from leaking. This water was frozen, and froze up the roller on which the pendants were wound, so the boat would not start, and I was frightened of losing sight of the schooner during the delay. However, we hooked the tackles, cut the pendants from the davits, and got her down.

The captain of the schooner came on board, and for fifty pounds agreed to pilot the ship to Halifax.

The bargain was no sooner made than the weather cleared, and away we went, steering N.N.W., and got to anchor off Halifax dockyard at 7 P.M.

I was considerably puzzled, as we got in, with the land, as I had not been accustomed to deal with land covered with snow, and I had to depend entirely on the pilot, but as he seemed to have every confidence in himself, I felt quite satisfied that he would take us up all right, which he did.

By the time we got to an anchor, the poor man was quite knocked up with the cold, and we had to put him to bed well wrapped up in hot blankets; we also administered hot soup, and what he seemed to relish most—hot whisky-and-water.

We found the 'Persia,' from Liverpool, commanded by the famous Captain Judkins of the Cunard line ; and the 'Arctic,' Captain Nicholson, from Southampton had arrived that morning. The ormer had succeeded in landing his troops at Three Rivers in the St Lawrence, but had been overtaken by the ice and obliged to abandon his boats, together with their officers and crews, and make a run for it. By landing his troops at Three Rivers, he had gained the Government reward of £1000, which the Cunard Company were generous enough to give to the captain, and place the honour the ship gained as an off-set to the loss of the boats.

Fortunately nothing happened to the officers and men, and they rejoined the ship, travelling overland for that purpose.

The ' Arctic ' had tried to get the Guards, whom she had on board, landed in the St Lawrence, but did not succeed, and they were still on board when we arrived.

I then learnt that one regiment was senior to another, and we had to take a second place at eight o'clock, when the Guards' drum and fife band played. Our drum and fife band had to wait till the other had finished. By that time our poor boys were very cold, having been kept standing ; and when their turn came, they did not play to please the drum major, who began to lay about them with his cane.

He severely dealt with one poor boy and made him cry, who in his grief said,—'How can you expect a fellow to play when his spittle freezes as fast as it goes into the fife.'

The thermometer was twenty-one below zero at the time.

The next day was spent in making arrangements for landing the troops. The Guards were not to land in Halifax, but were to go on to St John's, New Brunswick, as soon as land-transport could be provided for them.

CHAPTER V.

WITH the usual wonderful arrangements of the Admiralty in transport matters, as recorded in the earlier pages of this history, the Land Transport had been embarked in the slowest vessel they could find, and instead of arriving in time to serve the troops on landing, the 'Melbourne,' with them on board, did not turn up for a week after the regiments. When she did arrive, she was a wonderful sight. She was down two feet by the head with the weight of ice on her forecastle and about her bows, and presented quite a picture when the sun shone on it. They had had a very hard time on the latter part of the passage, and had only just enough coal to fetch in.

Our regiment was landed the next morning after breakfast, and their quarters were allotted in the citadel. On the march from the dockyard to the quarters eleven men fell out, and, lying down by the roadside, drunk from having taken too much liquor named 'Fixed bayonets,' were frozen to death, so fearful was the cold.

Our Artillery were not landed at Halifax, but remained on board. The Royal Engineers were transferred to the 'Arctic' and went on to St John's, New Brunswick.

I applied to the dockyard for coal, but there was none to be given me, as there were only 600 tons on charge, and that was reserved for the Royal Navy.

I was, therefore, in hopes I should be kept at Halifax for some time, as I could not go without coal. However, H.M.S 'Orpheus' came in, and the captain of her ordered me one day's coal (which took four days to put on board), and with what I had left I was to proceed to St John's, Newfoundland, land the Artillery, and go back to Sydney, Cape Breton, and coal for England from the mines at that place.

I accordingly left, and had for a passenger the celebrated Judge Haliburton (author of *Sam Slick* and other books), a very charming man, with, as we found, on arrival at Sydney, a very charming family.

We got safely to St John's, Newfoundland, after some little trouble on account of the ice, and found the harbour covered with ice about two inches thick. The town was in a state of mutiny, as there had been a row between the Roman Catholics and the Protestants, and the Royal Newfoundland Volunteers, when called upon by the Governor, refused to act.

Hence the Artillery were sent to disband them, and take possession of the citadel which commanded the town. By some means or other, the major who was in command of the battery had been left behind at Halifax, and had not reached us by land, and the command thus devolved on the first lieutenant, who was a very young officer.

The Governor thought we should await the major's arrival before landing the men, as he imagined there might be some opposition on the part of the volunteers. Our agent of transports on board thought differently, and said his orders were that no time should be lost in getting the ship to Sydney, Cape Breton.

The men were to be landed at the jetty belonging to the Lever Line, and the harbour-tug was to be used, as I positively refused to take the ship alongside the jetty, fearing she might be taken possession of by the natives.

We accordingly began to disembark the next morning. The men had their firelocks loaded, and their pouches full of cartridges, and every preparation was made for a struggle.

The yard at the back of the jetty and the jetty itself were packed closely with men, but we did not notice any arms among them.

We ran the tug across the end of the jetty, and her paddle-box top was just level with the top of the jetty. The officers and sergeants were on the paddle-box, and as soon as the tug was moored, the order was given, ' Fix bayonets.'

There was no landing-room left on the end of the jetty, and it was necessary to make some, so the sergeant-major let the butt of his firelock drop on to the toes of the nearest man, and made him move back all he was able and then took his place. The officer pointed his sword at the stomach of the man standing next to him, who made a retrograde movement and then landed.

He addressed the crowd and explained to them if they did not clear the jetty he would give the order to his men to fire, and that would be the signal for the guns on board the steamer lying off the jetty to open fire also (the crowd did not know that we had no guns on board).

This caused a general retrograde movement and the jetty was cleared, and the men in the tug landed without molestation.

The yard, however, was still closely packed, and

although a lane from the jetty to the gate was opened, the officer was too good a soldier to let his men march through in column. He spread them out along the face of the water, got round the crowd, and then ordered them out of the yard. There had to be a little touching of bayonets, but gradually the yard was cleared.

By this time the two field-pieces had been landed out of the tug, hauled up to the gate, and were ready for action, if necessary. One was pointed up the street and the other down, and the order was given to clear the up street which led to the Citadel.

Some little demur was made to this, but the crowd thought discretion the better part of valour, and before 2 P.M. the people had gone to their houses, and the artillery men were in possession of the Citadel.

This is the last piece of warfare I have been engaged in, and I was very pleased that we had gained a bloodless victory; but it was only terminated so well by the wonderful exercise of patience and foresight on the part of the young officer, who had the conduct of a very difficult operation. His name was Lieutenant Price, R.A.

Having landed what stores were required, we left for Sydney, Cape Breton, to coal; it took a fortnight to take in sufficient to carry us across to

England, as we could not get near to the wharf. We were obliged to take a large quantity, as the coal was not of too good a quality.

Whilst at Sydney, we were most hospitably entertained by Judge Haliburton and the various members of his family who were located round about. They used to send sleighs into Sydney to fetch us out, kept us for the night, and sent us back again by the same kind of conveyance. We were, however, nearly getting frozen in, and I had at one time every hopes of this happening, but the naval agent I had on board was too watchful for me, and I was obliged to leave.

I had great difficulty in getting the ship's head round, when we were getting under way, as the ice was of considerable thickness, and it took a good deal of going ahead and astern to break up enough of the ice to make room for the ship to turn in. Of course we had the leadsmen, but they were not of much use, as their fingers were about frozen up. However, I inquired of one of them, a crabbed old quarter-master who gloried in the name of Dick Turpin, 'What water have you, Turpin?'—(he stuttered so much that he could hardly speak at the best of times)—and he sung out to the leadsman's tune 'Not a damned drop,' as his lead was lying on the ice alongside.

However, by perseverance, we succeeded in getting out of the harbour. Outside I met the ' Arctic,' bound in. This ship was more fortunate than I had been; she got frozen in, and had to remain from the middle of February to well into May, all the time in the Government pay at the rate of £4000 per month!

On the fourth day out we fell in with a heavy gale, commencing with the wind at E. and N., and backing round by N. to S.W. The gale lasted seventy hours, and the ship suffered considerably. The rudder-head carried away, and she took to leaking badly at the fore-end of her; so much so, that I feared she would have gone down with us. We had to use the bilge injection all the time, and the donkey-pump as well. I was very glad when we got to Spithead, which we did on thirteenth day from Sydney. We remained there two days discharging stores into dockyard lighters, and then went to Southampton.

As the ship required a good deal of refitting to make her again a passenger-steamer, I was not wanted in her, and the captain of ' La Plata' giving in, I was sent in command of her to the West Indies, and got back again just after my ship had sailed for Brazil. I thus got a bit of a holiday till she came back, the proper captain of ' La Plata' rejoining.

When the ' Magdalena' returned, I was again

placed in and sailed her for five voyages to Brazil and back. On the last voyage it was that I brought home the Comte D'Eu and his wife, the Princess Imperial of Brazil. We had very bad weather in the Bay of Biscay, and I again had fears of the ship going down with us, as she worked so much she drew the starboard discharge pipe away from the ship's side, and every time she rolled it under, vast quantities of water poured in.

When we arrived at Southampton, I told the superintendent I should not go to sea in her again, as she was not safe. He said,—'My dear fellow, we shall send some one else.' I answered, 'All right, sir, you are the resident manager, and when the ship has gone down, I shall be left to give evidence that the ship was unseaworthy!' She did not go to sea again; instead, she was sold to the ship-breaker near Vauxhall Bridge, and broken up.

I made two voyages to Brazil in the 'Parana,' and one in 'La Plata,' and by that time the two new ships built for the line were ready, and on 9th October 1865 I sailed in command of the 'Rhone,' a very beautiful screw - steamer, built by the Milwall Ironworks Company.

The change from the old style of ship to the new was much the same as one would experience if, having been in the habit of riding a cart-horse you were all of a sudden put on the top of a racer.

The 'Rhone' was to all intents and purposes a steam-yacht fitted with every modern improvement and convenience, and I was very proud of being her commander. She was not too successful on her first voyage, as we were much troubled with hot bearings, and could not run her at the top speed. Nevertheless, we made a much faster passage than usual, and the passengers were so pleased that they presented me with a valuable pair of diamond solitaire earrings for my wife to wear.

It was in this ship that the first surface-condenser went to Brazil, and H.M. the Emperor came on board and thoroughly examined it. Whilst he was in the engine-room engaged in the examination, I, of course, had to be in attendance, and I don't think I ever felt the heat so much. His Majesty, however, did not appear to turn a hair, as the saying is. When he had finished and was about to leave the ship, he said to me, 'Good-bye Caballero Capitan.' I did not know exactly what was meant, but that afternoon came off two military officers and presented me with the Order of the Rose, and the patent of it, signed by the Emperor.

This honour, although a high one in Brazil, was of no use to me as an Englishman, as the British Minister at Rio de Janeiro took particular pains to notify me, as soon as he heard of the presentation. It appears that no Englishman is allowed to wear a foreign order unless it is given for services in the battlefield, and then only by the express permission of Her Majesty the Queen!

I have no doubt I could readily have obtained permission, but I did not consider it worth applying for, such things not being in my line. I have, however, worn it on two occasions—once when I attended the Emperor's levee, and once when I had the honour of dining with Sir Joseph Savory, Bart., when that gentleman was Lord Mayor of London, and I was asked to meet the Elder Brethren of the Trinity House.

The order gives the rank of colonel in the Brazilian army. I was telling Lord Charles Beresford of this when he was a passenger in the 'Tagus' under my command, and his lordship was of opinion that I ought to wear cherry-coloured pants instead of blue ones!

In January 1866, having left Southampton on 9th, I encountered the gale in which the unfortunate 'London' went down, and the 'Rhone' got severely handled. I annex a newspaper extract which gives all the account necessary of this incident :—

'We were enabled, in our Saturday's paper, to

announce, says the journal referred to, the safety of
the Royal Mail steamship " Rhone," but it was
not until the arrival of subsequent intelligence from
Lisbon that the alarm which existed amongst the
families of the crew of the " Rhone " was allayed.
It appears that when passed by the " Saxon," the
two vessels were within hailing distance, the
" Rhone " reporting the loss of four port-boats, and
damage to the screw. It was, however, thought by
many on the deck of the " Saxon " that the
" Rhone's " loss related to the *crew*, and this gave
rise to fearful rumours in the docks, until the
number actually lost was fixed at sixteen. The
news of the arrival of the " Rhone " at Lisbon dis-
pelled all anxiety, as her commander reported all
well so far as passengers and crew were concerned,
the only loss sustained being four boats and two
horses, with sundry sheep pens, etc., placed *hors de
combat*. The " Rhone," it appears, was exposed to
the fury of the terrific gale which proved so dis-
astrous to the ill-fated " London," and could not
have been far distant from that vessel, when she
became the living tomb of all on board. The
greatest confidence was felt by all who knew that
the command of the " Rhone " was entrusted to
Captain Woolward, one of the best commanders
that ever trod a quarter-deck. A letter from Mr J.
M. Lloyd, the secretary to the Royal Mail Com-

pany, published in the *Times*, gives the following, extract from a letter received from Captain R. Woolward, commander of the "Rhone:"—"We encountered a severe cyclone on January 11, 1866, wind from S.E., veering eastward to north, in which, I am sorry to say, the two lifeboats on the port-side and the cutter were lost, the starboard-cutter and mail-boat damaged, the rails and deck furniture much injured, two horses killed, and one of the crew had his leg broken. I have never before experienced such a gale. The barometer fell an inch and 11.100 in twelve hours, going as low as 28.34, and, although the wind was fair, we were obliged to lie to for ten hours." '

On the 'Rhone's' return to England, it was determined to send her on the West India line, the sister ship, the 'Douro,' having been sent on 17th February. The 'Rhone' left on 17th March, and arrived at Peter Island, 30th. We did not have very pleasant weather on the early part of the passage, but still arrived out in time, with a very great saving in coal compared to the paddle-wheel steamers with which the line had hitherto been worked.

The transfer of passengers and mails was effected at Peter Island instead of St Thomas, as yellow fever was prevalent at that island.

Since I was last in the West Indies, the Company's general superintendent had been made a Knight of the Dannebrog by His Majesty the King of Denmark.

The superintendent was very proud of this honour, and flourished it about on all occasions. He wrote me a letter on my arrival, and signed it 'John Black Cameron, K.D.' In answer to the letter, I signed myself Robert Woolward, C. & R. Mr Cameron had never liked me, and so thought I was making fun of him, and wrote me a letter—to use a nautical expression—all smoke and oakum, demanding my reason for insulting him!

I replied, in the most modest way, that no offence was intended; that as he signed his letter with his new honour following the signature, I merely did the same. I was glad to find the King of Denmark had made him a Knight of the Dannebrog, but I must inform him that the *Emperor* of Brazil had also made me a Knight of the Rose, and that I had equally the right to place C. & R. after my name as he had to place K.D. after his. I also told him, when he came off to the ship, that neither of us had any right to do so. I did not receive any more K.D. letters as long as I had to do with him, but when he retired I found he called himself Sir John Black Cameron, and madame assumed the title of Lady Cameron. I saw them so named amongst the arrivals at one of the Isle of Wight hotels.

The 'Rhone,' after the transfer at Peter Island, was sent down to Jamaica with the mails, etc., instead of the usual intercolonial steamer, as it was difficult to coal her at Peter Island.

We returned to England by the same route, and had a fine and quick passage. As this was a kind of a trial trip, I was glad to find the directors were pleased with the result, and it was determined to keep both the 'Rhone' and the 'Douro' on the West India line, and send the 'Shannon' and 'Seine,' the large paddle-wheel steamers, to Brazil in their places.

CHAPTER VI.

I WENT a second voyage to the West Indies in the 'Rhone,' and had a bishop going out, and two on the way home, as passengers.

The homeward bound bishops were transferred to the 'Rhone' at St Thomas—one, Dr Selwyn, was the Bishop of New Zealand; the other, Bishop Harper, was the suffragan. The passengers who came across to Panama in the same ship complained to me it had been turned into a kind of conventicle, and expressed a hope that I would not allow the same thing to go on, as they had had too much of it. I told them they need not be alarmed, as we had so many foreigners on board and so many different religions.

The first Thursday we were out from St Thomas I found some practising of church-music and singing going on, on the fore part of the main deck. I watched an opportunity and asked Mrs Harper what was all the noise I had heard?

She said,—'Don't you know, we were practising for Sunday?'

I told her they need not trouble, for nothing of the sort would go on there on Sunday, as the service commenced at half-past ten and was bound to be over before eleven.

Later in the day, the Bishop of New Zealand said to me,—'Is it true, Captain, we sha'n't be able to have our usual choral service on board?'

'Quite true, my lord,' said I. 'My experience is against such things on board, and it can't be, except in the evening, as the crew have to change their clothes and have their dinners before noon; at all events, as many of them as have to go on watch at that time.'

The bishop began to argue the point, and it ended by my saying to him,—

'My lord, you forget that I am the bishop of this diocese, and I don't allow any interference with my prerogative.'

This ended the matter, and I had no more trouble with the church-party till we were approaching England. One morning the bishop (who thought he was a navigator, as he had been knocking about in the Colony in his schooner) came to me and said,—'Captain, I notice that you are steering S.E., and, according to my reckoning, we shall fetch Gibraltar.' 'All right, my lord,' said I, 'you keep a good lookout for the Rock, and let me know when you see it.'

The bishop cleared out for the time, but, having consulted with two ship captains, who were also passengers, he came back later in an inquiring mood. I then relieved his mind and told him the ship's standard compass had forty-six degrees of error on the course we were steering, and that we were making a course one degree north of east and should doubtless make the English land in due time.

Some years after I met the chaplain to the Bishop of Lincoln, and found that the then Bishop of Lichfield, Dr Selwyn, had frequently told the story and considered it a very good joke, being told by the captain of the steamer that *he*, the captain, was the bishop of that diocese, *i.e.*, the ship!

I did not go in the 'Rhone' any more. The captain of the 'Shannon' did not like the Brazil line, and, being my senior, claimed the 'Rhone,' and I was appointed to the 'Shannon.'

I was very much put out at this, but it will be seen that it was ordered for the best, as the 'Rhone' was lost on her next voyage, on 29th October, 1867. Very few were saved, and the captain perished.

There is one curious coincidence, too, attached to

the loss of the 'Rhone.' We had had a nurse in our family, and she got married to a fireman in the 'Rhone,' and when the news of the loss of the ship came, my wife went to break it to her former nurse. The young woman said,—'I knew it, but my Bill is all right, I saw him land in a dream; he went ashore from the wreck on a large, square-looking thing; he's all right.' And so he was. When the survivors arrived, her Bill was amongst them, and he had got ashore on one of the 'hammock binns'!

I had been in the 'Rhone' every voyage she had made till that one, and when she was lost I was safe on board the 'Shannon,' at Bahia, in Brazil.

On the way out, the second day after passing St Vincent, Cape Verde, a young lady died from rheumatic fever. Curiously enough, she died within very few miles of the place where she was born, having been born at sea on board H.M. Packet brig 'Petrel.' I did not bury her at sea. My valuable surgeon, Dr Hunter, embalmed the body, and we carried the poor thing round with us, and handed her over to her relations in England, who were very grateful to us for so doing.

We had the coffin stowed in a house on the fore-side of the bridge, and I was obliged to let the third officer keep watch all day, as nothing would persuade him to remain on the bridge after dark.

On the way home we had a bad breakdown of the starboard engine, the day before we arrived at St Vincent, and we had to perform the rest of the passage with the port engine; fortunately, no one was hurt.

The wind being ahead all the way to Lisbon, I got somewhat behind, and only arrived off Plymouth on the day I should have been at Southampton.

I accordingly put into Plymouth, landed the mails, telegraphed to Southampton for a tug to meet me at the Needles, and went on. I got safely into Southampton Dock the next day.

Owing to the loss of the 'Rhone,' the Company bought the contract for building the 'Neva,' by Messrs Caird of Greenock, and I found the captain of the 'Douro' had been sent to superintend the finishing of the 'Neva.'

I was appointed to the command of the 'Douro,' and sailed in her on the West India route again. Instead of merely going as far as St Thomas, and returning thence to Southampton, the route was now extended to Colon, the Atlantic port from which the Panama Railway started. This was owing to the increase of traffic over the isthmus, brought about by the railway convenience. I would have taken too long to transfer the through cargo at St Thomas as before, besides which, passengers from Peru, etc., objected to the change of ships.

We had to remain fourteen days at Colon under this arrangement, as we always arrived out just as the homeward steamer was leaving.

As it was the season of the Northers at Colon, I did not remain there, but went up to Porto Bello, a secure harbour about twenty miles to N.E. of Colon, and the proper place for the Panama Railway to have started from, as there was the old Spanish road to Panama still remaining, and in not very bad order.

As soon as the Panama Railway scheme was talked of, some American speculators bought up all the land about Porto Bello for a mere song, and then put such a price on it that the Panama Railway Company shifted their line to Colon.

As matters turned out, it would have cost much less to have bought the Porto Bello land, as the railway had to be carried mostly through a swampy country, and fever carried off thousands of labourers ; so much so, that it was said that a labourer was buried at each end of each sleeper !

I don't believe that any one ever knew how many *did* die ; all I can say is, that during the time I was employed on the Spanish Main route and the line was being made, I used to carry 300 labourers each month from Carthagena to Colon, and certainly never carried more than twenty back, and the other ship in the month did about the same. I have even taken men in at Colon, and they have died before we arrived at Carthagena, the passage only occupying thirty-six hours.

In the spring of 1869 the 'Douro' was again placed on the Brazil route. We sailed on 9th April, and I was laid up a great part of the voyage with rheumatic fever, but I had the consolation, during the whole time, of knowing the ship was being well taken care of by my chief officer, Mr Ebenezer Kemp, who commanded the ship later on, and went down with her when she sank from collision with a Spanish steamer. A better officer or a kinder man could not have been found any-where.—*R.I.P.*

On the next voyage we were full of passengers, both out and home. One night, on the way out, the weather being very hot, it was necessary to leave the lower-deck scuttles open, contrary to the Company's regulations. I am aware, however, they were left open.

One of the cabins abreast the engine-room was occupied by a Portuguese family with several children. Most of them were sleeping on the deck of the cabin, and there was a light left burning in

the light-room of the cabin. Towards 1 A.M. a
flying fish flew in through the scuttle, dropped
amongst the children, and floundering about,
frightened them considerably, and they began to
scream.

The neighbouring people rushed out to see what
was the matter, and, not being able to find out,
started screaming also, and the ship got into a
terrible state of commotion. I went down below,
but could not get along the passage for the crowd,
and I had to do a good deal of fighting before I
could reach the cabin. By this time the author
of the mischief had been discovered, but not till
the passengers in general had become fully per-
suaded that, at least, the ship was on fire, if not
sinking. I have never known a greater scare in a
ship than that one.

On the way home we brought His Serene
Highness the Duke of Saxe, who had married the
second daughter of the Emperor. They had a
young family, and their eldest boy, about seven or
eight years old, was about the grandest Turk I
ever came across. They simply could do nothing
with him in the way of control. He had the bump
of mischief most strongly developed, and it ran in
the direction of throwing everything he could get
at overboard! The first object of his attention in
that way was a large bunch of keys belonging to

the baggage. Next in order was the contents of the picnic-basket—the basket itself would not go through the scuttle. Hair-brushes, tooth-brushes —all went to Davy Jones.

There was a raffle got up for a model of the ship, and the gentleman who won it presented it to the young scamp, who sat and admired it for some little time, and then threw it down on the deck and jumped on it till it was quite broken up!

On arrival at Lisbon, or rather at Belim, we were, as usual, placed in quarantine.

The king came on board in his state-barge to call on the Brazilian princess, and her husband. The visit over, His Majesty was about to leave the ship. I stopped him on the top of the gangway and pointed out the yellow flag at the fore, and told him he would not be able to leave the ship, or we should be fined for breach of the quarantine law.

His Majesty was very angry, and said,—'Captain, I will never come and see you again.' I said,— 'Your Majesty, you did not come on board to see me; it was the princess you came to see.'

He sent his barge ashore and the health officer came off and released the ship. His Majesty then left. I expected the health officer would put us back into quarantine after the king was clear, but he did not.

I had known the king when he was a midshipman in the English Royal Navy. He had made two passages in the ship under my command.

When the Duke of Saxe left the ship, he presented me with a handsome ring, set with red, white and blue stones, being a ruby, diamond and sapphire, and the princess gave me a single-stone diamond ring.

The other passengers also made me a present of a handsome tea and coffee service, so I may say I made a very good voyage.

The next and last voyage I made to Brazil, we were sent down to open the River Plate route. Hitherto, passengers from Monte Video and Buenos Ayres had to change into a smaller vessel at Rio de Janeiro. As the Messagerie Imperiale Company sent their large steamer through from Bordeaux to Buenos Ayres, the Royal Mail were compelled to do the same, or they would have suffered considerably in their passenger traffic.

We were very well received at Buenos Ayres, and a public dinner was given to mark the occasion. We sat down at seven o'clock, and at two the next morning the doctor of the 'Douro' and myself left the table, but we were the first to do so. I can't say when the talking came to an end, but I was told it went on some time longer.

We left Buenos Ayres in the evening, 14th November, and arrived at Monte Video early the next morning. Here we found that Madame Ristori, and her company, were to be amongst our passengers.

Notice had been given of a performance to take place that evening, but it was the proper day for the ship to leave. The naval-agent ordered the consul to have the mail ready at 6 P.M. He said the ship would have to wait till the next day, as Madame Ristori's performance had been advertised and must take place. After some interchange of civilities between these two gentlemen, the consul said he would not give the mails, and the naval-agent said,—' In that case, I shall sail without them.'

Madame came off later in the day, and tried to induce the naval-agent to remain, but her fascinations were not sufficiently powerful. It is needless to say the mails were delivered at the time ordered, and the ship sailed, the naval-agent observing,—' Whoever heard of Her Majesty's mails being detained to please a play-acting woman?'

Of course, all the way home Madame would have nothing to do with the naval-agent, whom she always spoke of as a *bête noir*.

At Rio de Janeiro there was a grand performance given by Madame as her farewell to Brazil. Tickets were sent for everyone on board—passengers, officers and engineers; only the naval-agent was left out. I did not go, but sent all my officers except one, and handed my ticket over to the naval-agent, but he would not go.

In the middle of the performance, at which the emperor, empress and all the grand people of the place were present, there was a grand to-do. One of the ladies, when called on, was missing, and could not be found anywhere. The telegraph was set to work, and the chief of police ordered, by His Majesty, to see to it, and a grand fuss in general was made.

It was found the lady had eloped with the captain of a Brazilian frigate, and the frigate had gone to sea. Here was a dreadful scandal. I think Madame Ristori might have congratulated herself that the young lady had waited till the tour had come to an end, and not gone off before. She was exceedingly handsome, and the prima donna. The captain carried off a prize, and I hope he has treated her well. We heard of her marriage, at Rio Grande do Sul, later.

CHAPTER VII.

NOTHING startling occurred on the passage home till after we had passed Finisterre, when, in a strong N.W. wind, the fore-topsail-sheet carried away, and the sail made a great noise before we could get it clewed up. The passengers were very much alarmed, and I went down to the fore part of the main-deck to reassure them. I found Madame Ristori in a great flutter, and, as I went towards her, she put her arms round me and fainted off, as if she were dead. I had heard of her doing this on the stage, but had not seen it, and found I was acting the part of the villain in the play, who bring about this dreadful ending in the tragedy, for which Madame was famous.

In January of 1870 I was appointed to the 'Neva,' and permanently fixed on the West India line, at least, as the appointment stated, 'during the pleasure of the Court of Directors.' It will thus be seen that I had no guarantee of tenure of office beyond the one voyage.   I and my brother officers have always been under the same unsatisfactory kind of agreement, and are still.   We are liable to be discharged at any time, after the ship completes her voyage.

On this first voyage in the 'Neva,' I took my youngest child, eight years old, with me.   He had been suffering from whooping-cough, and for two winters too, and there were threatenings of its coming on again.   He went the round voyage with me, and, after a few days out, all the bad symptoms had disappeared, and he returned thoroughly se up.   I mention this to show the great benefit to be derived from a sea voyage, particularly in such ships as those of the Royal Mail Steam Packet Company.   They are replete with comfort and convenience, although, possibly, they don't make the show the ships of some lines do.   I have seen, in my experience, hundreds of sick people brought on board at Southampton, many of whom could not even walk, and before we got out to West Indies they have improved wonderfully, and before arrival back to England have completely recovered.

I am always telling folks of the poor man who had to take seven dips in the river Jordan before he could get cured, whereas only one trip in the Royal Mail Company's rivers (all the ships are named after rivers) is required to set them up completely.

N.B.—Don't look upon this as an advertisement; it is merely good advice, and much better than doctors'.

The ordinary route to Colon was, by this time, extended, and the Atlantic steamer, instead of remaining at Colon for the fortnight, went on to Carthagena and Sta. Marta once a month, and once a month to Greytown. This was a great improvement, as our crews used to get very sickly lying at Colon.

Nothing worthy of note occurred on the passage out, but I was much frightened at the chance of losing my child at Sta. Marta. He was very fond of going away in the boats, when they went, and one afternoon the doctor and the Jamaica pilot, Dowie by name, with two lads, went away pelican shooting, in the ship's dinghy.

The child was mad to go with them, and I in a weak moment consented. At nightfall the breeze came down very strong, and the boat could not pull up against it. They made sail on her and commenced threshing her up against the wind and sea, and the last thing I saw of the boat, just after sunset, was that she was standing off shore on the starboard tack, and I did not fancy she could live much longer in the sea that was getting up.

My feelings can be better imagined than described, from the time darkness shut in and 8.30 P.M., when the boat fetched up to the ship, all right.

After all my anxiety, when I embraced the child, he said,—'Had such a splendid sail, daddy. Didn't she give us a wetting? The doctor and I had to keep baling all the time, whilst Yeo and Johnson laid in the bottom of the boat for ballast.'

I said to him,—'Who sailed the boat, then?' He answered,—'Dowie, of course, as the doctor did not know anything about it.'

At St Thomas, homeward, the late Canon Kingsley and his daughter came on board to go to England. As the passage is so fully described in the canon's book, *At Last*, I need not attempt it.

I was very glad when we got home and I was able to hand my dear boy over to his mother, safe and sound. The boy learnt more on the voyage than he would have done in a year ashore, and that without looking at a book all the time he was away.

Nothing occurred on the next voyage, and it was not till August the monotony was at all broken. This was my third voyage in the ship, and we left Southampton on 17th August, and had fine weather till the morning of 29th, when I became aware we were approaching the path of a hurricane, and at 2 P.M. I rounded to on starboard tack.

I annex the extract from the newspaper, as the best account of it that can be given.

This was the first occasion I had had of thoroughly appreciating the kindness of Sir William Reid, in instructing myself and the other officers of the old 'Medway' in the law of storms, as mentioned in the earlier part of my narrative.

It is a pity the commander of the 'Martinique' had not had the same advantage. I had a very pitiful account of his experience of it from the passengers of that vessel, who were transferred to the 'Neva,' to be carried on to their destination, the 'Martinique' not being able to continue her voyage. One said to me, *'Figurez vous, monsieur, trente-six heures sans nouriture.'*

The following is an account of the hurricane in the West Indies referred to, during 1870. The newspapers wrote :—

'By the arrival of the Royal Mail Company's steamship, "Elbe," Captain T. A. Bevis, which reached Southampton on the Sunday night, we learn that the "Neva," belonging to the same Company, and commanded by Captain R. Woolward, which left Southampton on the 17th of August with the West India and Pacific mails, experienced a severe hurricane on the 29th and 30th, about 450 miles N.E. of St Thomas. The circle of the hurricane was about 360 miles; it travelled in a north-westerly direction, and the southernmost edge swept past Sombrero. The utmost damage about the Virgin Islands, so far reported, was the driving ashore of the smaller boats by the strong wind and heavy swell. It is to be feared, however, that in the vast extent which the hurricane would travel over, probably as far as to the north-west of Bermuda (if not across the Atlantic to the European coast) many ships would be caught, and many disasters take place; some to be reported, and some never to be heard of except in the brief notices, appearing from time to time, of "missing ships." Early on the morning of the 29th, the "Neva" fell in with a strong breeze, and the baro-meter began to fall, though not rapidly at first. By noon, however, the indications of a coming tempest had developed. Sails were lowered, boats secured, everything made tight, the ship hove to, and the result awaited. The wind came whirling, roaring, rolling, with as terrible a sea as ever human eye beheld. Captain Woolward calculated from the force and direction of the wind and the sea, according to the theory of hurricanes, that the centre of the storm lay directly across the course of the "Neva," and he hoped, by laying to, to escape the worst.   The event proved the correctness of his judgment.   After twenty-four hours of anxious waiting and terrible tossing, the ship was able to make headway slowly, and by the morning of the 31st the wind and sea had gone down.   The French steamer, " Martinique," which arrived at St Thomas a few hours before the " Neva," had her fires put out and her boats washed away, and seven feet of water in her hold.   She had one of her crew killed, and a passenger died from fright ; she only got out of the storm as if by miracle.   On the morning of the 1st September, as the " Neva " was nearing St Thomas, the passengers presented Captain Woolward with the following address :—

'" ON BOARD THE ' NEVA,' OFF ST THOMAS,
Sept. 1st, 1870.

'" Dear Sir,—As we are now so nearly approaching the end of our transatlantic voyage, we are unwilling to separate without writing to assure you of the feelings which have been called forth by your great judgment, forethought and skill, to which, under the good providence of God, we believe we owe our preservation under circumstances of no ordinary anxiety and danger.

'" We beg, dear sir, to offer our hearty thanks to yourself and the officers and men under your command for the admirable seamanship which you all exhibited during the tempestuous weather we experienced, and the imminent danger which threatened us on Monday and Tuesday last.

'"Wishing you to retain some memorial of a voyage which we ourselves can never forget, we beg your acceptance of the accompanying purse, which, although conveying a very inadequate expression of our feelings, we hope you will lay out in some abiding token of the debt of gratitude which we owe to your skill.—We remain, dear sir, yours very truly."

'(Here followed the passengers' signatures.)

'The purse contained £25, 10s., and the captain was requested to have the following inscription placed on whatever he might purchase in commemoration of the event:—"From the passengers of the 'Neva' to Captain Woolward, in appreciation of his skilful seamanship during a hurricane on the 29th and 30th August, 1870."

Captain Woolward, in reply, expressed his satisfaction at such a kind appreciation of his services. He must, however, disclaim any extraordinary merit in following the course which he adopted. Thanks were due to the Almighty Power who had, in His mercy, revealed sufficient of His laws to enable His creatures to avoid a danger, probably necessary to keep up the balance of the atmosphere, for their good. The credit of this discovery was due to a soldier, and not to a sailor. It was now happily possible, in most instances, for the commander of a ship, by the exercise of ordinary foresight, and by careful attention to the indications of the barometer and the course of the wind, to avoid the worst fury of a hurricane, although, if once drawn within its vortex, the best ship became unmanageable. Then human efforts were powerless, and the finest seamanship was unavailing, as was shown by that mournful monument which they were then passing (and he pointed with his hand to the masts of the ill-fated "Rhone," which at that moment could be seen from the cabin). In acknowledging the compliment paid in the address to his officers and crew, he said that much was due to their merit and skill, and remarked that the Company had taken great pains to get together, and keep, skilled officers. He wished the passengers a happy arrival at their several destinations, and concluded by saying,—"Let us all thank God for having brought us safely past a great danger."

' The following is the memorandum from the commander of the "Neva":—"August 29th, at 3 A.M., barometer had fallen 1-10th since 10 P.M., 28th. At 10 A.M., no rise of barometer and no fall. At noon, barometer 29.94. At 2 P.M., barometer 29.74. Laid to under close-reefed top-sails and fore-topmast staysail, on starboard tack. Cyclone centre, S.W. 100 miles, strong gale and heavy sea; Sombrero, S. 52½, W. 376 miles. At 4 P.M. 29th, barometer 29.76 and wind S.E.; ship's head E.N.E. At noon 30th, wind S.S.E., barometer 29.90; set on slowly to S.S.E. till 4 P.M., and then kept on course; gale decreasing, but with heavy sea from N.W., S.W. and S.E. At 8 P.M. 30th, barometer 29.98, and stars out. The 'Neva' was laid to for twenty-two hours; not the least damage done to her, and the passengers subscribed 150 dollars for a silver barometer to Captain Woolward for the prudent, judicious, and masterly manner in which he managed his ship."

'The following is the account of the commander of the "Martinique":—"Nothing particular in our navigation up to the 28th. In the night of the 28th to the 29th our position was lat. 19.30 N., long. 62.10 W. The barometer was going down with rapidity, and announced that we were in the course of a cyclone. At six o'clock in the morning of the 30th barometer was 7.55, the puffs of wind very violent from N.N.E. At eleven o'clock the barometer was 7.44, wind very strong, and the sea covering the steamer lying off and on. At ten o'clock barometer was at its lowest point, 7.38. We were in the centre of the cyclone when the lull came on, and it lasted up to three o'clock. The sea was very heavy. At three o'clock the wind came again in terrible puffs from S.W.; laid to without sails or steam, our fires having been extinguished by a sea we shipped. At four o'clock the cyclone was in all its force. The barometer began to go up. The tempest continued up to three o'clock in the morning of the 30th. The barometer went up to 7.55, and the weather moderated."

'Sea disturbances and other indications of the storm were experienced at Barbadoes, Antigua, St Lucia, and other places to the northward, but no damage had been heard of on sea or land.'

On this voyage we went to Greytown, so called after Earl Grey, under whose administration it, as the capital of the Mosquito Coast, was placed under British protection.

There was a very fair harbour there up to 1857, but at the time I am writing about it had nearly filled up, and only very small craft could get in.

Early in 1857 I was inside in the R.M.S. 'Thames,' and at the same time, H.M.S. 'Tartar,' 'Cossack,' and a despatch gunboat were at anchor, besides two steamers of the Nicaragua Transit Company (American).

Between that and the spring of 1858, the place

had nearly filled up, owing to the washing away of an island that was situated at the fork of the San Juan and Colorado Rivers.

This island belonged to, and was inhabited by, a family of the name of Leaf, very worthy, industrious people.

One night, I never was able to get the exact date, the river became very much swollen with the heavy rain up country, and the whole island was carried away ; with it went the Leaf family and all their belongings.

Nothing occurred till we were on the passage home and arrived at Jamaica. There we found the outward mail steamer was overdue, and as we should have, of necessity, to wait at St Thomas till the intercolonial steamer came back, the superintendent, a worthy old port captain of Her Majesty's navy, decided to keep us for the benefit of the Jamaica community.

It so happened, during the time, there was a sale by auction of the goods and chattels at one of the houses just outside the town.

Now, a sale by auction in the West Indies is a very different thing from a sale by auction in England. A good luncheon is provided, and plenty of liquor served out, and the bidding goes on, to say the least of it, very merrily.

At this particular sale, one item was a prettily-trimmed 'bassinette,' and it was knocked down in a lot to a gentleman who did not want it.

As the superintendent had bought some things, his cart would be sent to take them home, and it struck some of the party (of course, *I* was not one of them), that a rise could be taken out of the superintendent, who was a confirmed old bachelor, by means of this bassinette.

Accordingly, when the cart was loaded, the bassinette was put on top, and half-a-crown given to the driver to go home by way of Harbour Street, and stop for a little time to rest his horse opposite the Commercial Rooms.

This he managed very cleverly, and arrived at his resting-place exactly at one o'clock, when folks were going in to luncheon.

Naturally, seeing the old captain's cart with a bassinette on it, they came to the conclusion he was at last going to be married, and sent in cards of congratulation forthwith.

It appears the old gentleman had been in the habit of proposing to a buxom widow once a year, for some years, and receiving the cards from so many people, began to think, somehow or another, that the widow had said 'yes' and he had not understood her.

Accordingly he went to inquire of the widow what it all meant?   All the answer he got was, ' No, you old fool, but I don't fancy, even if we were to get married, you would have any need of a bassinette.'

He went away cursing (so the story goes) and saying, 'That's that d—d fellow Woolward again.' Possibly he was not so far out.

The superintendent had seen much service in the Royal Navy, and on one occasion got tried for his life.

He was the lieutenant of the watch in a frigate lying at Spithead and ready for sea. Orders had been given that no boats should be allowed alongside, as there had been some desertions amongst the crew. One gentleman of the Hebrew persuasion still hanging about, notwithstanding the order, and probably giving vent to his opinion in language more forcible than polite, the lieutenant gave the sentry orders to fire at him, not for a moment supposing the musket was loaded, except with the blank cartridge which would be wanted at sunset.

The man fired, and killed the Hebrew, to the astonishment of the sentry, if not of the Jew, who had not much time to form an opinion.

Of course here (to use marine parlance) was a big row on, and when the matter was reported to the port-admiral he was equal to the occasion, and ordered the frigate to sea, 'to look for a privateer said to be cruising 700 miles west of the Lizard.'

As they were not likely, at that date, to find such a thing as a privateer, in due time the frigate returned, the lieutenant was arrested, tried and acquitted, having been defended by the smartest lawyer of the day.

Doubtless, had the admiral not been smart and got the frigate out of the way, and kept her away till popular opinion had subsided, it would have gone hard with both officer and marine.

The superintendent lived in the enjoyment of his office to a good old age. Such a man ought, if possible, to live for ever; his life was employed in doing good to others, and I never heard anyone speak evil of him.

He had a wonderful parrot, which lived in the gallery of his house. This parrot, when he heard anyone narrating, waited patiently till the finish of the story, and then said, in a loud voice, 'That's a lie.'

When it was announced in the house that the poor old captain was dead, the parrot said, as usual, 'That's a lie.'

Possibly Polly was right. Who knows?

CHAPTER VIII.

WE arrived home in due time after a favourable passage, and then I was transferred to the command of the 'Tagus,' a new ship built by Messrs John Elder & Company.

I was very proud of my new command, as she was a fine ship of the most modern type, but after enjoying my appointment for a week or so I was taken out of her.

The 'Elbe' had left Southampton on 2d June 1871, but, owing to an accident to her machinery, returned on the 3d, and it was determined to transfer the passengers, cargo, officers and crew to the 'Tagus,' and place the captain of the 'Elbe' in command.

This transfer was effected in twenty hours, and the 'Tagus' left, on the afternoon of 4th June, and saved her contract time out to West Indies.

The repairs to the 'Elbe' were completed by the middle of the month, and I sailed in command of her on 17th June.

We had a fine passage out, as was to be expected at that period of the year, but, on arrival at Jamaica, we found the 'Tagus' had failed to get any further on her voyage than there, so we took on board the cargo, etc., for the Spanish Main, and went on with it and our own.

I made a second voyage in the 'Elbe' and had my second experience of a fire on board ship,

We arrived alongside the wharf at Colon on the afternoon of 23d September, and commenced landing the cargo.

At Jamaica two puncheons of rum had been put on board. These were too large to go into either of the lock-ups, and had to be stowed on the after orlop deck.

The cargo work aft was being superintended by the mate of the hold, and he, poor man, was induced by some of the crew, who were at work under him, to broach one of the puncheons of rum.

The story told by one of the men, who got severely burnt, was, that the mate of the hold bored a hole in the head of the cask, but the rum would not run out into the pannikin, as it had no vent. He then bored a hole in the top of the cask, and, as soon as that was done, the rum blew out all over him and the lantern, 'and that's all I know about it,' said the man.

Fortunately I was close at hand, and as soon as

I noticed the flames coming up the after hatch, I had the hatches put on and covered up. My staunch friend, Mr Young, the chief engineer, turned on the steam fire-annihilator, and in about ten minutes the fire was out.

The mate of the hold, however, was burnt to death, and two other of the men were badly burnt. One cask of the rum was consumed, and seven cases of snuff that were stowed close to it were burnt, but that was all the damage, except to the stores in the steward's storeroom. Here all the hams were cooked, also the bacon and cheese, as I had the steam kept on in the orlop-deck till midnight, to make sure the fire would not break out again.

This was the first ship in the Company's service that was fitted with an annihilator, and I can vouch thoroughly for their efficiency.

Turning the steam on and pumping water down at the same time is a mistake, as the water only condenses the steam. I have never since had any fear of fire in the hold, as the steam will master it at once.

Since that time, whenever I have had rum as cargo from Jamaica to Colon, I have seen it landed as soon after arrival as possible, and for a long time after I would not allow it to be put below. I had it stowed on the quarter deck and looked after by the junior officer of the watch. When, however, the Panama Canal Works were going, we carried it in too large quantities for this to be done, and it had to be stowed below again.

This voyage I called at Sąvanilla for the first time.

The railway from there to Barranquilla having commenced running, the cargo was beginning to find its way down to Savanilla instead of going to Sta. Marta as formerly.

Savanilla is a much nicer place to remain at than Sta. Marta. The nuisances of sand flies and mosquitoes do not exist, and there is generally a nice breeze blowing.

On the passage home, the only fact worth noting was the experience of the effects of a submarine volcano, or, at all events, of such as I judged it to be.

When we were in lat. 30 00' N., and long. 53° 00' W., at 0.45 P.M., 18th October, we observed a large volume of water thrown up at least 150 feet, and rollers spreading from its vicinity in all directions. As the sea was till then, and had been, smooth, there were no fiddles on the saloon tables, which were spread for luncheon, consequently, when the rollers struck the ship, everything was thrown off the tables and all the glass and crockery ware broken. I should say £50 would not have paid for the damage.

I made one more uneventful voyage in the 'Elbe,' and then left her. I was very glad to be clear of her, as at that time, owing to the heavy way in which she was rigged, I did not consider her quite safe when she got lightened of her coal nearing England in the winter time.

The Company soon had this defect remedied, and now the 'Elbe' is a very nice ship, and, to my fancy, one of the prettiest in the service. She is beautifully fitted up, and looks like a nobleman's yacht on a large scale; she is most comfortable to travel in and fairly fast.

By giving up my stay at home, I was enabled to get the command of the 'Tagus,' and left Southampton on 2d November, 1871. I made fifteen voyages in her, most of which were uneventful.

On the earlier voyages we were much troubled with the slide valve of the high pressure cylinder.

It was from the giving in of this valve that the failure of the ship's first voyage was brought about. She was obliged to remain at Kingston, Jamaica, till a new face was fitted to it.

When she got home, an entirely new valve was fitted, but, fortunately, they did not land the old one, as the new valve cut its face out on the fifth day after leaving Southampton, and it had to be taken out and the one refaced by the engineers of the ship at Jamaica substituted.

This amusement went on for some voyages, the Southampton valve giving in about the fifth or sixth day out, and the ship stopped for about four hours till we could get the original one put in.

The whole defect was caused by there being a hinge between the slide valve and the piston guide above it, and as soon as the chief engineer was allowed to have his way and make the valve spindle and the guide-rod continuous, we had no more trouble with it.

It was during the time we were struggling with this valve that I came to the conclusion that sails would be of no use to the ship in the case of a breakdown, as long as the propeller was left.

All the time we were stopped, the ship would remain with the wind abeam and no other way, sail or no sail. I had her under full sail on one occasion for thirty-six hours, with a fine, fair breeze, and tried everything I knew of to keep her on her course, but she would only lie with the wind abeam, making, at right angles to the wind, about two miles per hour.

Ever since I have been an advocate for not only doing away with the sails in a steamer, but with the masts also, as I consider them only an expensive and useless luxury.

Any good they may do when the wind is fair, is more than counteracted when the wind is ahead.

In a fourteen knot steamer the wind will be ahead, or before the beam generally.

I notice all the new-fashioned steamships have very little masts, and I fancy, if it were not for clinging to the idea that the thing would not be a ship without masts, none would be put.

In my opinion, a steamer does not want masts any more than Noah's Ark did. The constructors of H.M. modern battle ships seem to have the same idea.

I carried in the 'Tagus' the largest number of saloon passengers I have ever carried at one time, viz., 402.

This occurred from an accident to one of the Compagnie Générale Transatlantique Company's ships.

The superintendent at St Thomas, very wrongly, to my mind, transferred the passengers from the French steamer which had broken down, to the 'Tagus' at St Thomas, forgetting the ship would most likely be filled by our own regular clients at Barbadoes.

The consequence was, an overcrowded ship and much discomfort to everyone.

I had to fit up sleeping berths all over the ship, and to be out of my cabin at six o'clock every morning, to allow ladies to use it as a dressing-room.

The passengers on this occasion were very good to me, and put up with their discomfort without complaining, and without getting me fined for carrying more passengers than I was licensed by the certificate to carry.

I take this opportunity of thanking them; possibly some of them may read this history and recollect the time as vividly as I do.

My connection with the 'Tagus' was broken by a collision between us and a small brig off the Lizard, the end of November 1874.

We had passed the Lizard and made the usual night signals, and I considered the officer of the watch (the second officer) could safely be left in charge for a short time whilst I went below to put on some warmer clothes, as a bitter N.E. wind was blowing.

I had not left the bridge five minutes, when I noticed the engines stopped and reversed.

On going out of my cabin I saw a small brig pass close to us, but could not see anything wrong with her.

I went on the bridge and asked the second officer if he had touched the brig. He said 'No,' he had not been any nearer to it than I saw as she passed. We, therefore, went on our course.

The brig did not make any signal of distress, so I concluded that what the second officer told me was correct.

A day or two after we arrived at Southampton, being the 1st December, 1874, I received notice from the Board of Trade Office that we had run down a brig and proceeded on our voyage without rendering any assistance.

I am still of opinion we did *not* touch the brig, and that her sinking has to be accounted for in some other way.

One thing is certain, and that is, the brig was forty years old, and the captain of her was half owner ; the brig was, also, fully insured.

There was a Board of Trade inquiry, and the 'Tagus' was found liable, and the Royal Mail Company had to pay for both the brig (160 tons) and her cargo of coal.

It appears the brig had her stern to us, so her lights were shut out from our view.

There was no rule, at that time, that a vessel should show a light astern, as now, that an over-taking ship should be able to keep clear of her. I conclude that our accident (if it may be so termed) was the cause of the rule being made, as the magistrate at the Greenwich Police Court, before whom I was brought up, observed, 'He thought the brig should have showed a light, as he was bound to have seen a ship like the "Tagus," lighted up like a street, coming on to him.'

I may here say, the case in the court immediately preceding ours, was a young gentleman brought up for breaking lamps in the street the previous night. He was fined five shillings for being drunk, and cost of lamps, etc.

Evidently the British Government of that day thought that breaking street-lamps and breaking up ships were in the same category. I wondered they did not fine us the five shillings, as well as ordering us to pay the costs of the brig and her cargo.

Fancy a police magistrate being considered the proper judge of cases of shipwreck! They might just as well make me a judge in the Ecclesiastical Court!

This inquiry was not ended when the 'Tagus' was to sail on 17th December, and another commander had to be appointed.

Whilst the inquiry was pending, I was sent down to Liverpool to bring the 'Corcovado' round to Southampton.

This ship had been bought by the Royal Mail Company from the O.S.N. Company. She had been built by those princes of shipbuilders, Messrs

Laird Brothers, of Birkenhead, and was now to be placed on the West India line.

As it turned out, my leaving the 'Tagus' was very much to my advantage. As had been the case in several other instances, the 'Tagus' came to grief soon after I was out of her.

She sailed under the command of my old chief officer, Ebenezer Kemp, and whilst lying alongside the Company's wharf at Colon, with everything on board for the homeward voyage, except the mail, she was run into by the Royal Mail Company's ship 'Severn,' and sunk.

She was afterwards raised, repaired and came home, but it cost the Royal Mail Company all of £30,000, to say nothing of the inconvenience to everyone on board of her. Several of the crew took fever, and one of them lost his reason and has never recovered it.

CHAPTER IX.

EARLY in January 1875 I was appointed to the command of the ship I had brought round from Liverpool, now called the 'Don,' and we sailed on her first voyage on 17th January.

She was the first ship I had sailed in that had steam steering apparatus, and was the second ship of the Royal Mail Company that had it. The first was the 'Para' (formerly the 'Puno'), sister ship to the 'Don,' also bought from the O.S.N. Company and built by the same builders as the 'Don.'

I made sixty consecutive voyages in the 'Don' to the West Indies, and, with the exception of two, made good and pleasant passages out and home.

The first of these exceptions was in September 1880, when we had to round to, to allow a cyclone to pass ahead of us.

'The cause of the detention in the arrival of the mail was due, we understand,' says the newspaper in question, 'to the severe weather which the "Don" encountered on the ocean passage; luckily the long experience of Captain Woolward enabled him to detect the approach of the storm, and, to a certain extent, avoid it. The accompanying letter, with a purse subscribed among the passengers, was presented to the captain; we also publish Captain Woolward's reply :—

'" ROYAL MAIL STEAMER ' DON,'
30*th Sept.* 1880.

'" ROBERT WOOLWARD, Esq.,

'" Dear Sir,—As passengers of the ' Don,' under your care, we desire, before leaving the ship, to express our sense of obligation to you for the kind care and ceaseless watchfulness that have ministered to our comfort and safety.

'" We are not unmindful of the fact that your long and honourable career as a captain in this service renders any testimony of ours of little value.

'" But it is a duty to you, and one we owe to ourselves, that we should especially record our gratitude to you for the decision of character, the firmness of purpose, the skilful seamanship, and the vigilance with which every point of danger was guarded in the terrible hurricane through which we have passed.

'" The presence of these essential qualities of seamanship in you has, under the kind hand of God, been our safety—the lack of them might have been our ruin.

'"As an expression (but very inadequate one) of these sentiments, we desire your acceptance of a purse (£30), and with it a wish that every blessing which comes from His Fatherly hand, 'Whom winds and seas obey,' may be yours.—We are, dear Sir, yours faithfully,

'"(Signed by 90 Passengers.)"'

[*Reply.*]
'"ON BOARD THE 'DON,'
30*th Sept.* 1880.

'"Ladies and Gentlemen,—I have to thank you very much for the kind manner in which you have expressed your satisfaction of the passage in the good ship under us.

'"Although so old a commander, I take much pleasure in receiving so handsome a testimonial from you, and trust I may for some time longer be spared to minister to your comfort and safety.

'"With regard to the storm, which we to a certain extent avoided, my great experience of the weather in these seas enabled me to detect the approach of it long before the instruments which science has placed at my service gave any indication; in fact, they only did so four hours before it commenced. The first notice I got of atmospheric disturbance was on Sunday morning, when a landrail flew on board, the ship at the time being 1200 miles from any land.   The same circumstances having occurred to me ten years ago, when I saved the 'Neva,' then under my command, from the fearful discomfiture experienced by another steamship within a few miles of her, and who 'ran on' instead of 'rounding to' as she should have done.

'"On that occasion I was presented by the passengers on board with the best barometer that could be bought, and they possibly will have the satisfaction of learning that their gift has been of great service to you and many others.

'"There is still an instrument I am short of, and the purse you have so kindly added will be used to furnish it.   On its face, if you have no objection, I shall have placed a similar inscription.

'"Wishing you all you can possibly wish yourselves, and hoping again to have the pleasure of ferrying you across the Atlantic, allow me to subscribe myself,—Yours faithfully,

'" ROBERT WOOLWARD, *Commander*."'

The newspaper account of it I annex, but we never were in the storm, or within 200 miles of its centre.

We were, however, quite near enough ; in fact

too near to be pleasant, though the ship was never in the slightest danger; but the fact that the hatches were battened down, and every precaution taken in case worse weather came on, made the passengers fancy they were in danger.

The second occasion was a far more serious affair, and the ship really had a narrow escape, for had she shipped a second such sea like the one described in the newspaper account, the fires would in all probability have been put out.

Fortunately nothing of the kind happened, and in the afternoon of the day, 21st October, 1881, the gale began to abate, and on the morning of 22d we were enabled to get the steering-gear fixed up and make better way, but it was not till the 24th October we were able to go full speed, as the sea was so heavy.

'TERRIFIC GALES EXPERIENCED BY R.M.S. "DON" ON HER OUTWARD VOYAGE FROM SOUTHAMPTON TO BARBADOES, BY A PASSENGER.

'This fine ship left Southampton waters on the 17th October, at 3.30 P.M., with fine weather, having on board a large general cargo—mails for the West Indies, 213 first and second-class passengers, and a crew consisting of 123 hands, all told. Every one on board seemed to turn into bed in excellent spirits that night. The next day (18th) the wind increased to a moderate gale, from S.S.E., with high sea. At 1 P.M. the ship was taking in water fore and aft.

'19th, 1 A.M. Wind increased to a strong gale, ship taking in large quantities of water on deck, and at 3.30 A.M. violent squalls and rain split fore-top staysails; all passengers terribly alarmed, ship rolling fearfully.

'20th Oct. No change whatever, great anxiety prevailed on board. At 6 A.M. commenced to rain, accompanied with violent squalls and wind veering to west, sea mountainous and ship rolling terribly, passengers' chairs and trunks being pitched about in every direction, while the breaking of crockery and other articles on board was sufficient to unnerve the stoutest heart.

'21st. Oct. Strong gale blowing, ship pitching and taking in water; 2 A.M., vivid lightning, St Elmas lights all over rigging, heavy rain; 4 A.M., gale increasing and sea rising, furious squalls at times; 11 A.M., steering chain carried away, ship falling off the sea, shipped a heavy sea in the main rigging, carrying away engine pen, skylights, deck-houses, ventilators, two boats (and seriously injuring a third), and doing other severe damage; also injuring the captain, officers and several of the crew. The captain, while working away amidst the confusion surrounding the steering apparatus, was knocked down and his right arm dislocated, but, singular to relate, while he was being supported by the Honourable Mr Burford Hancock, the ship made a heavy lurch, when the captain caught hold of something to support him, and, in doing so, his arm slipped back in its place again. Just at this time there were two and a half feet water in the engine-room, and it was thought, if two more such seas were shipped, the ship must be swamped.

'It would be impossible to describe the fearful condition of passengers and, indeed, all on board, just at this time, the storm being now at its climax, while every soul in the ship anticipated a watery grave. To add to the horrors of the situation, an alarm of fire was now raised, and a general panic ensued. A large quantity of smoke, or steam vapour, it appears, found its way into the forward saloon, where many of the lady passengers were anxiously awaiting their fate; and this circumstance seemed indeed to verify the report that the ship was on fire. Happily, however, we were spared from such a terrible catastrophe. A little later and another alarm, no less terrifying, was raised, viz., that the ship was sinking. This was equally justifiable, for a part of the skylight over the after-saloon was smashed in, and great volumes of water came rushing in, apparently on all sides.

It can easily be imagined how this report was received. The passengers became almost frantic with fear and excitement, and the piercing shrieks of the ladies made the bravest heart quail. By this time, however, through the indefatigable energy and bravery of our good old captain, officers and crew, the steering apparatus was temporarily secured, and steering was resumed by the aid of wire hawsers and tackles, and in this way we proceeded on our voyage till next day.

'22d Oct., 1 A.M. Heavy gale and high seas, ship labouring and taking in large quantities of water on deck, fore and aft.

'4 A.M., wind moderating; 5 A.M., connected stearing gear; 8 A.M., strong gale and very heavy sea, main-stay carried away; secured mast with wire hawsers; 12 A.M., heavy gale and high seas, with furious squalls, ship rolling heavily.

'23d, Sunday, 1 A.M. Strong gale and heavy squalls, high seas and ship labouring fearfully, taking in much water over all. 6 A.M., wind moderating. 8 A.M., strong gale again, and squally; all hands had to be employed in cleaning up wreck about the decks, securing balance of boats, etc.

'11 A.M. Passengers assembled in saloon, where Divine Service was held, the captain officiating. Directly prayers were over, a committee was

formed, and a resolution passed, to open a sub-
scription list to raise a fund for captain, officers
and crew, in recognition of the valiant conduct
and indefatigable energy which they displayed
during the whole time. At 8 o'clock P.M.,
barometer commenced to fall and gale increased,
as before. At noon were 200 miles north-west of
St Michaels (Azores). Sighted the island at 1.30
P.M. on the 24th (next day) for a short time, after
which it was obscured by rain. Directly the ship
rounded the island the sea increased again, ship
pitching heavily, had to ease the engines. When
the ship was 600 miles off the Azores, the captain,
considering the danger that the ship and all on
board were in, decided to run into the port of St
Michaels as a place of refuge. The passengers, I
need hardly remark, were delighted at this; but
on the sea and rain moderating — when we got
nearer to the island—the captain, after dinner on
Sunday evening, explained his reasons for not
wishing to call at that port, and it was unanimously decided not to do so, and to trust to the
captain's judgment, in proceeding right on to
Barbadoes.

'I cannot conclude these hurried notes without
making mention of the gallant conduct of many
of the gentlemen passengers during the trying
catastrophe that I have just imperfectly described.

It would be, indeed, invidious to particularise any six or eight gentlemen, but I am sure that the ladies, whose spirits were so often cheered and fortified by the *gallantry* and *bravery* of these gentlemen, will not object if I at least mention the names of the Hon. J. B. Burford Hancock, Antigua; Mr Nicholas Cox, inspector-general, police, Demerara; and Mr A. Douglas P. Owen, inspector, police, Trinidad, whose valiant conduct cannot be too highly estimated and will long be remembered by all who were on board.

'Meeting of Passengers on Board.

'A meeting of the passengers was held on Sunday, 23d October, when it was unanimously resolved that, in view of the great peril from which the passengers have been delivered during the storm of Friday the 21st instant, by the exertions (under God's blessing) of Captain Woolward and the ship's company, it is suitable that some substantial mark of their sense of those exertions should be presented by the passengers to the captain, officers and crew, and that with this object subscriptions should be collected.

'The following gentlemen were appointed a committee to carry the resolution into effect: —Sir David Chalmers, chairman, Demerara;

Victor Griffroy, Esq., Antigua ; B. Handley, Esq., London ; S. N. Collymore, Esq., Barbadoes ; Hon. H. J. Burford Hancock, Leeward Islands ; T. R. St John, Esq., Central America ; Dr Galgey, St Lucia ; B. Howell Jones, Esq., Demerara ; Robt. S. Cheeseman, Esq., St Vincent ; N. Cox, Esq., Demerara ; G. Agard, Esq., Tobago ; D. M. Gallagher, Esq., Demerara ; F. Blakely, Esq., Tobago ; Newburn Garnett, Esq., Demerara ; A. D. Owen, Esq., Trinidad ; E. J. Henry, Esq., Demerara ; G. Grant, Esq., Trinidad ; A. B. Agacio, Esq., Guatemala ; F. C. Scott, Esq., Trinidad ; J. W. Parkins, Jamaica ; Rev. J. Hartell, Jamaica ; M. Poux, Esq., Hayti ; — Fabrey, Esq., Colon.

'The following gentlemen were appointed to act as a committee for the purpose of receiving subscriptions :—N. Cox, Esq. ; A. D. P. Owen, Esq. ; B. Handley, Esq. ; A. B. Agacio, Esq. ; R. M. S. Cheeseman, Esq. ; D. M. Gallagher, Esq.

'On Sunday, the 30th, all the passengers, officers and crew were summoned on the quarter-deck, when Mr Nicholas Cox, of Demerara, in a clear voice, read the following address and handed Captain Woolward and officers the amount of the subscriptions, amounting to £202. The captain returned thanks for himself and on behalf of the other recipients in brief but appropriate terms :—

'" To Captain ROBERT WOOLWARD, the Officers and Crew of R.M.S. ' Don ' :—

'" Gentlemen,—We whose names are hereunto subscribed, passengers on board the Royal Mail steamer ' Don,' on her present voyage from Southampton to the West Indies, under command of Captain Robert Woolward, desire, before the arrival of the ship at her first port of destination shall lead to our separation, to express our gratitude to Captain Woolward and his officers and crew, by whose exertions, under the favour of Almighty God, we were delivered from great peril of shipwreck during the very severe storm which raged from 1 o'clock P.M. on the 18th of October, until noon on 23d, culminating on Friday 21st of October current. The most imminent danger was caused by the breaking of the steering gear and the staving in by the sea of the covering of the engine-room and of the companion of the after-saloon when the gale was at its height. By the skill and promptitude with which Captain Woolward gave orders for temporarily repairing those all but vital injuries to the ship, and the ability, courage and devotion to their duty with which officers and men seconded the efforts of their captain, and continued to navigate the ship throughout the storm under great difficulties, in which some severe personal injuries were received by men and officers, the ship and lives of all on board were saved.

' " Where all behaved so well there is difficulty in mentioning any names except that of the captain ; but we feel confident that the ship's company will think with us, that peculiar praise is due, after Captain Woolward, to Mr Joseph Bunting, chief officer ; Mr Joseph Cottier, second officer ; Mr Robert Major, chief engineer ; Mr William Howell, third engineer ; Edward Sheath, carpenter ; John Wren, boatswain ; and John Hopkins, mate of the hold ; who all were led, by the course of their duty, during the critical period, to have prominent parts in the measures which were taken for the common safety.

' " We have collected amongst ourselves a sum of £202. This collection in no way measures, and was not intended to measure, our feelings of gratitude (which are not capable of being measured by a money standard), but merely as giving a tangible expression—however slight and in-adequate—to our feelings. Of this sum we beg that Captain Woolward will accept forty guineas, with the view of expending it on any article he may think fit, to be preserved as a memorial of the peril and deliverance of this voyage ; that the officers will accept £95 in the following proportions, viz. :—Mr Bunting, Mr Cottier and Mr Major, £20

each; Mr Banks and Mr Howell, £10 each;
Edward Sheath, John Wren and John Hopkins,
£5 each, with the view that each of them also may
procure some memorial of the like nature, and that
Captain Woolward will distribute the remainder
of the money, amounting to £65, in such proportions as he may consider most suitable, amongst
such of the rest of the ship's company, including
the head and other stewards, as, in his judgment,
contributed by their exertions to the saving of the
ship.

' " On board Royal Mail S. 'Don,' 30th day of
October, 1881.

' " (Signed) David Patrick Chalmers, Chief Justice,
British Guiana; F. K. St John, Minister in C.
America; B. Howell Jones, Demerara; A. B.
Agacio, Consul of the Argentine Republic, Guate-
mala, C.A.; Robt. S. Cheeseman, Member of
Executive and Legislative Council, St Vincent;
Otho Galry, medical officer, St Lucia; J. W. Par-
kin, J.P., St James and Hanover, Jamaica, and pro-
prietor of estates; M. Garnett, Demerara; Dennis
M'Gallagher, Asst. Govt. Secretary, Berbice and
British Guiana; J. Watt, Consul for Spain and
Italy, Trinidad; Henry J. B. Burford Hancock,
Lieut.-Governor, administering Government in Chief,
Leeward Islands; George Grant, Trinidad; John
Hartell, Jamaica; S. N. Collymore, Barbadoes; A.

Douglas P. Owen, Inspector of Police, Trinidad; Nicholas Cox, Inspector-General of Police, British Guiana; H. Burford Hancock, Sternden, Andover, Wilts and Antigua; Alice Gordon Grant, Trinidad; Emily S. Briggs, Barbadoes; Ethel A. Freeling, Trinidad; K. Garnett, Demerara; Edmund Meney, British Guiana; Benj. Handley, engineer, London; W. M. Farnum, Barbadoes; J. Howard Bayley, Barbadoes; W. B. Farnum, Barbadoes; Carl Schock, Trinidad; D. Nivin, Demerara; D. O'Reilly, J.P., Jamaica; Thos. Smart, Glasgow; D. M. Simpson, Barbadoes; Thomas Blakeley, Tobago; F. W. B. Ward, Jamaica; and about one hundred other names." '

It was on this voyage I had on board the first of the people who went out to commence work on the Panama Canal—the greatest swindle that has been since George Law's Mississippi Scheme.

The party consisted of forty-four, mostly Belgian mechanics, a very rough lot, but they were very useful to me in making temporary repairs after the storm. I don't think any of them lived to return to their native country.

For the next five years the principal business of the ship was to carry people to Colon for service on the canal works.

On more than one occasion I have landed

over a thousand people at Colon. Negroes flocked there from all parts of the West Indies, attracted by the promise of high wages.

Jamaica was the place which contributed the largest number, and that island reaped great profit from the transaction in the end, although the planters and others were much inconvenienced whilst the work was being carried on.

Of course many of the Jamaicans died, but much the larger number returned with sufficient money to enable them to become small settlers on a bit of land of their own.

However, I doubt if one-tenth of the white mechanics that went out from France and Belgium ever returned. The mortality was terrible, notwithstanding every possible hospital accommodation was provided, and the best medical attendance was at hand.

I often wondered how the Frenchmen were induced to accept service on the 'isthmus,' as I can vouch for their being in great fear of the climate all through the passage outward.

Amongst the number who went out in the 'Don' on one particular voyage, was a correspondent of the *Nouveau Monde Illustré*, and as we were nearing the West Indies, this good man began to get alarmed, and fancied he was going to die of fever. He came to me and inquired what we did with a person who died on the voyage. I answered,—'Why, throw him overboard at once.' 'Don't you think, captain, that is a very dreadful thing to do?' 'No,' said I, 'I don't; for, if you die and are properly buried at sea, you have a light burning over you all the the rest of time.'

He said he never knew it, and went away in a very doubtful mood, thinking possibly he would sooner not die, even with the light thrown in.

Nothing more passed on the subject, but I was determined not to allow him to fancy I had misinformed him. So, a few days after, I told him that, about eight o'clock this evening, we should be passing the place where I buried a passenger two years ago, and that we might see whether the light were burning or not.

I arranged with my chief officer that, just before eight o'clock, he should have one of Holmes' life-buoy lights thrown overboard from the bowsprit end; that, as soon as it ignited, the lookout man forward was to call out—'Corpse light on the bow,' which he did. The lookout man on the bridge sang out also—'Corpse light on the port bow.' Up rushed the passengers, the Frenchman amongst them, and there, lo and behold! was the 'corpse light' they had been led to expect, but did not believe in.

The Frenchman was fully convinced, and prepared a very elaborate account of the occurrence for his newspaper, which was duly published.

He brought the account to me to read, and when I pronounced it correct, he wanted me to sign it. I told him I could not do that, as the Royal Mail Company did not allow their officers to have anything to do with newspapers, except to read them. He said,—'Captain, may I put that you would have signed it, but for this reason?' and I said,—'Certainly,' which satisfied him. The account duly appeared, and I had the pleasure of reading it.

The poor man was travelling with his son and a clever French poodle. I landed them at Colon in due course, as also the party of sixty-two who were in his company. I returned to England, and when I arrived alongside the wharf at Colon on the next voyage, a term of only ten weeks having elapsed, the dog came on board, and took up his quarters, he being the only survivor of the sixty-four who had landed with him.

I have known men fresh out from France sent to work on the steam navvies in the morning, struck with the fever before night, and buried the next day.

The heads ot the various departments did not fare any better, neither did the doctors or sisters

of mercy who worked in the hospitals. What between malaria and absinthe, grim death had it
all his own way.

All the time the work was going on, there was
no kind of amusement to divert the men's minds
when the day's work was over, and gambling and
drinking were the only means of passing the time
in the evening.

When the work shut down, it took several ships
to bring away the West Indians, and re-convey
them to their homes, but as far as the 'Don' was
concerned, we only had about one hundred Euro-
peans to carry back. Of course. many others went
in other ships and by other lines, but the per-
centage was very small compared to the number
that went out.

An event occured to the 'Don' between Jamaica
and Port-au-Prince, which thoroughly proved the
staunchness of the ship.

We left Kingston at 8 A.M., 10th May, 1883, and
towards 11 P.M. the same day, were close up towards Jeremie, a town in Hayti, when a steamer
was sighted coming towards us, on the starboard
side, and having his green light to our green light,
and by all rules of the road at sea, both ships were
to keep their course, and in an ordinary way would
pass clear of each other.

Suddenly, I missed sight of the other vessel's

green light, and saw only his masthead light and was somewhat puzzled. However, very shortly after, I saw his green light again and at the same time distinctly made out that he had shifted his green light from his starboard side to his port side, and was endeavouring to run into us.

Instantly I shifted my helm to hard a-port, and so averted a catastrophe to the 'Don,' but not so to the other vessel. We came into collision, my stem striking him on the broad of his starboard bow, and his stem striking me under the starboard cathead.

He began to sink at once, and just had time to back close in shore and get his stern on the ground, but his bows went down in deep water, drowning all his engine-room crew and 130 Haytian soldiers.

Had I not made up my mind in good time what his intention was, viz., to ram me on the starboard side, and let him have my stem instead of letting him give me his, the chances would have been that he would have sunk me instead of my sinking him. As it was, he made a small hole just below the water line in my ship, filled the collision compartment, and cut out the side of our boatswain's store-room, making a hole twelve feet by eight feet, but doing no material damage.

We lowered our boats and went to look for him,

but did not find him, as he had been smart enough to back away to the shore. But we concluded he had sunk.

In the compartment next to the collision compartment we had 3700 bags of coffee stowed, and as the filling of the collision compartment had brought the ship's bows down to the twenty-five feet mark, I determined to shift the coffee aft, and we put the whole of the crew on to the work at once, the engines remaining stopped all the time.

By daylight in the morning we had brought the hole out of the water, and were able to pump the water out of the collision compartment and proceed to Port-au-Prince, where we arrived safely at 2 P.M the day after the collision.

Here I found one of Her Majesty's ships, the 'Griffon,' and reported the circumstance there, and also to Mr Carew Hunt, H.B.M. Consul.

This was on the Friday, and on the Sunday there arrived in Port-au-Prince the captain of the vessel with which we had collided.

His account was that he had seen a steamer coming up, and took it for the one that had been sold by the Royal Mail Steam Packet Company to the party who had started a revolution to depose General Saloman, the President. This vessel when in the Royal Mail service was called the 'Eider'; her new owners called her 'La Patrie.'

The vessel we had collided with was 'Le Renard,' a small cruiser belonging to General Saloman's Government, and was on her way round to Aux Cayes, a town on the south side of Hayti, with troops to reinforce the garrison of that place.

The captain of 'Le Renard,' considering the 'Don' was 'La Patrie' on her way up to relieve the town of Marrgaone, determined to destroy her in his capacity of a Haytian man-of-war.

As he had no guns, he concluded the best way was to run into her, and was very much astonished to find he had caught a tartar.

Nevertheless, when he arrived at Port-au-Prince, minus his vessel, he posed in the line of a great patriot, gave out he had sunk 'La Patrie' and all on board, and otherwise represented himself as a hero.

Mr Hunt, the consul, hearing this account, got this patriotic gentleman into his office, asked him to give him the account of the transaction, and his shorthand writer took it all down as he narrated it.

When he had finished, Mr Hunt said to him,—

'Perhaps you are not aware that it is known up here, that, instead of your having sunk 'La Patrie,' as you assert, you attempted to sink the British mail-steamer, and that the captain of her was smart enough to detect your purpose, and so sank your vessel instead. The "Don" is now at anchor in the harbour, and I shall, on the morrow, make a claim on your Government for £10,000 to cover the damage done, and the delay to H.B.M. mail steamer.'

We were delayed at Port-au-Prince till the Tuesday evening, when, by the help of the mechanics from the British man-of-war and our own, we had riveted iron patches on the hole abreast our fourteen feet mark, and covered in with wood the hole in the boatswain's store-room.

The officers from the man-of-war surveyed the ship, and we proceeded on our voyage, and arrived at Plymouth not very much behind the contract time.

As we were long overdue at St Thomas, our port of call between Port-au-Prince and Plymouth, and the superintendent had not heard of us, he sent the R.M.S. 'Solent' off with the homeward mail at 10 P.M. the night before we arrived, instead of waiting —as he should have done—for forty-eight hours after the contract time for sailing had passed, and so put the Company to much unnecessary expense, as well as leaving the station short of a ship.

The 'Don' arrived at St Thomas at 8 P.M., and the forty-eight hours were only up at 10 P.M. the same night. I was anxious to go on for Plymouth at once, but he would not permit me. As there was

no reason for detaining me, I arrived at the conclusion he did it to allow the 'Solent' to get sufficient start so as to arrive home before the 'Don'
could.

If this was his reason, he was foiled, as I put the
'Don' to her speed and we arrived at Plymouth
long before the 'Solent'; indeed, we arrived at
Southampton before the 'Solent' got to Plymouth.

On arrival at Plymouth, the captain of the
'Solent' said to the Company's agent,—

'Alas! the poor "Don," nothing had been heard
of her for some days before I left St Thomas; no
doubt she has gone.'

'The "Don?"' said the agent, 'why, the "Don"
arrived in Southampton some hours ago!'

One thing I regretted in the above occurrence, was taking the trouble to save the coffee,
which was removed from the forehold. It cost us
a good deal of labour, and the underwriters took no
notice of the exertions made in their behalf. It
would have been much easier to have dumped it
overboard.

In January 1882 what I have since called the
'Battle of Port Royal,' took place, and in which the
'Don' was the vessel engaged.

At that time the command of the military in the
West Indies was held by a general whose head-
quarters were at Barbadoes, and twice a year he

went on a tour of inspection of the Leeward Islands, part of his command.

Sometimes he would go down to Jamaica in a man-of-war, but more frequently he took passage in the mail-steamer.

By the Queen's regulations, when the general is afloat, he hoists a certain flag, which is a British Union Jack with a device in the centre. The Union Jack at the fore is also the signal for a pilot in English ships, but a merchant ship is obliged to have a white border to the Union Jack, and if one of them should fly the flag without a border, the flag is liable to be seized by any man-of-war who comes across it, and the ship is also liable to a penalty of not exceeding ' Five hundred pounds.'

On this occasion, as we were nearing Port Royal, with the general on board, his aide-de-camp sent the flag up and requested me to allow it to be hoisted at the fore as usual.

There was a very crusty old gentleman as commodore on the station. The sailors always said of him that the last time he had been in action he had his starboard - main - topgallant rigging shot away, and that was the reason he always went about with his head listed nearly down to his port shoulder.

Jack has generally a curious way of accounting

for things, as everyone who has had much to do with him knows.

Whether the commodore took the general's flag for the contraband Union Jack or not I can't say, but when the 'Don' arrived at Port Royal, he sent his coxswain, with the officer of the guard, to haul the flag down and seize it.

The officer came on to the 'Don's' bridge with the Merchant Shipping Act under his arm, and told me he had orders to haul down the flag from the fore, and seize it. I said to him, 'Go ahead; there will be a fine lark over it. Don't you know it is the general's flag and that he is on board?'

The general was down below dressing at the time, but his wife represented him at the gangway, and protested, in the general's name, against what she was pleased to call the outrage to the service. However, the flag went away, and we went on to Kingston without it.

This led to a *contretemps*, as the commanding officer at Kingston, not seeing the general's flag flying as usual, thought the general was not on board, and did not come down to the wharf to receive him, and there was no guard of honour.

As soon as the flag was hauled down I 'smelt the battle from afar.' We had on board at the same time an admiral going out to take command on the Pacific Station. This officer had been the commodore at Port Royal immediately before the present one, and knew that the flag was rightly hoisted, and that there would be what he called 'a jolly row about it.'

When the officer handed in the general's flag to the commodore, it was discovered to be a *bona fide* Queen's flag with the Government mark in it, but the old gentleman determined to stand to his guns and not admit he had made a mistake, or he might have got out of the difficulty, as the general was a very kind man and unpretentious.

Having got the flag into his hands, the commodore did not know what to do with it. It was military stores, and he had no more right to have it than I had. However, he sent it back to the 'Don,' but I would not receive it. He sent it up to the ordnance office. They would have nothing to do with it, so the dockyard folks had to hold it, waiting orders.

A few hours after we got to Kingston I received a letter, 'all smoke and oakum,' as the saying is, from the commodore, inquiring why he should not fine me 'five hundred pounds.'

I am pretty good at writing letters, and here was a grand opportunity. I explained to the commodore 'that he could not fine anyone;' at the outside, he could only bring the case into the law court, and if he wanted to be thoroughly laughed at, I should advise him to start off at once, and I wound up by saying that, in my opinion, the whole affair was what might have been expected had Mr Midshipman Easy been acting commodore, and that I fancied he would find running into the biggest merchant vessel he could find was a very good way of bringing his ship to an anchor like Mr Midshipman Easy.

This turned out to be the case; the commodore invalided and so saved a court-martial. The flag had to be hoisted at Port Royal, and saluted, and then returned to the general.

I continued in the 'Don,' making the same voyages till she had made sixty-one; that is to say, had crossed the Atlantic 122 times and run 671,000 miles, when a new contract was about to be made with the Post-office, and an increase of speed demanded.

It was decided to place the ship in the hands of Earle's Shipbuilding Company at Hull, and have her modernised.

We therefore left Southampton for Hull on 30th July, 1888, and delivered the ship over on 31st.

I was transferred to the 'Nile,' a very old ship, and one that was not at all equal to the service required of her, but she was considered one of the strongest ships afloat, and was comfortable.

She was a caution, certainly, to have anything to do with. Short of speed from her birth, she could not carry either the coal she burnt or the cargo that offered. We always arrived after time, and were obliged to remain longer in port than the time allowed to get the little cargo she carried in and out, as her hatchways were too small, and her cargo gear very much behind the times.

The only good thing about her was the saloon galley, and that was the best, by a long way, with which I had been shipmates.

However, I made eight comfortable voyages in her, and it was quite an amusement to have to flog her along and make her arrive in some sort of time to save the post-office fines.

I arrived at Barbadoes on 15th October, 1889, which was exactly forty-five years from the date of my first joining the Company.

The passengers were pleased to celebrate this event in my life, as they termed it, and presented me with a handsome letter, signed by eighty-three persons, and a purse containing thirty guineas, to buy a minute-repeating watch on my return to England.

In May 1890 I regained the 'Don,' now made a fine ship of in every way; her speed increased two knots, and her general accommodation much improved, as well as her safety in bad weather. I was very much pleased with the ship, and much gratified at being reappointed to her.

The only drawback to being in such a ship is the monotony of the voyages, one of which is exactly like the other. The only variation is in the weather, and that in itself does not vary much. As a rule, after passing the Azores, fine weather is experienced throughout till arriving back on the homeward voyage to the same latitude.

In the West Indies the weather is generally fine, and I can't understand how anyone can complain of the climate. To my fancy, nothing can be more pleasant than the weather experienced out there, except, perhaps, in the rainy season, when it is rather steamy during the day, but in most parts the nights are cool.

The great drawback to all tropical parts is the want of twilight. It gets dark very shortly after the sun goes down. This is in some measure compensated for by the lovely moonlight evenings, which are most enjoyable, and if the moon only carried out its orders, and ruled the night as the sun rules the day, there would be nothing more to be desired in these parts.

The routes of the mail steamers in the West Indies, of which there are five on the main line, and three on the intercolonial, are worked quite as regularly as any railway in England.

The main line ships leave Southampton every other Wednesday, pass the Azores on their way out on the next Sunday, and arrive at Barbadoes shortly before 6 A.M. on the Monday week; so regular are they, that the people in Barbadoes say they can set their clocks by them.

At Barbadoes they meet always the three inter-colonial steamers; one going to Demerara, one going to St Vincent, Grenada, Trinidad, Tobago, and La Guayra, and the third going to St Lucia, Martinique, Dominica, Guadaloupe, Antigua, Mont-serrat, Nevis, St Kitts and St Thomas.

The Demerara ship leaves Barbadoes generally at 2 P.M., but sometimes earlier on account of saving the tide into George Town. This ship has always the preference in the transfer of mails, passengers and cargo, as she is the only one that is troubled with tide.

Demerara considers itself 'The place on that side of the water,' and is about the only place the directors of the Royal Mail Company have not been able to satisfy.

The other two intercolonial ships leave Barba-does in the evening and are not in a hurry, as the next ports at which they call are only a short run, and can easily be reached by daylight on Tuesday.

The passengers for these two vessels have, therefore, a whole day to spend on shore at

Barbadoes, which is as much time as is required to see all there is to be seen.

The island, arriving early in the morning, presents a beautiful appearance, particularly to new-comers to the Tropics after having been at sea for twelve days, and not having seen anything possibly the whole time, beyond two or three ships.

The Azores are not always seen, although the ships generally pass within thirty miles of them, and the route out to Barbadoes is not the route taken by sailing-ships. Sailing-ships are sometimes seen on the Wednesday after leaving Southampton, as the mail-steamer arrives on that day at the point on which the track of the homeward bound sailing-ships, which have come round either the Cape of Good Hope or Cape Horn, also that of those bound to Europe from the coast of Brazil to the eastward of Cape St Roque crosses the track of the mail-steamer.

The Atlantic steamer also leaves Barbadoes, on her way to Jacmel, Jamaica and Colon, at five or six o'clock on the same Monday on which she arrives, and her passengers have a full day to visit the island, as they have not the trouble to transfer themselves and their goods to any other ship.

My advice to them, however, is not to go on shore till after they have had their breakfasts, except they have friends to receive them, as the hotels are not prepared for an influx of visitors early on a Monday morning. Passengers who are strangers in the West Indies, and have not a friend's house at their disposal, will do well to accept the fact that the Royal Mail steamer is the best place round about at which to get a square meal.

I have heard people say a change is a good thing sometimes, even if it is a change for the worse, but I always go on the principle,—' Let well alone,' and I find it generally answers.

The Atlantic steamer having left Barbadoes at nightfall, passes between St Lucia and St Vincent soon after midnight, and enters the Caribbean Sea, and generally finds herself in fine, smooth water, teeming with flying fish. The water will keep smooth all the Tuesday, but will become rougher on the Wednesday as the ship gets out from the lee of the Windward Islands.

This is the hottest part of the voyage, as the wind is right aft and mostly blows at the same speed as the steamer runs, and folks who have come out for the trip, begin to wish themselves back again ; but it soon passes, and as the approach to the Haytian land is on the Wednesday evening, when the wind comes off the land, they get cool again.

Towards midnight on the Wednesday, the ship

passes a rocky islet called Alta Tela, at present uninhabited.

Some few years ago an American Company rented Alta Tela from the San Domingo Government, and set up works for procuring phosphate of lime on the west side of it.

It was not very long before they ran short of provisions and water, and the larger number, including the headman, left in the schooner that tended them, to fetch a supply. They were much longer gone than was expected, and those that remained were getting starved. They made a raft, having no boat, and started with a view of getting on to the mainland ; they have not since been heard of.

When the schooner returned, she found the island deserted, and a paper left to inform them of what had happened. Operations were not resumed.

On the Thursday morning, about half-past six, the steamer arrives at Jacmel, and sends her boat on shore with the mails.

Whilst the boat is away, the few passengers for the place and the small amount of cargo are put into native boats, and such passengers as are going away in the steamer are taken on board.

The water is too deep for the steamer to anchor, so she drifts about the bay.

The view from the steamer is the best part of

the proceeding; some few passengers have, from time to time, gone ashore in the mail boat, but the time is too short to allow them to see anything. Mr Froude, in his book entitled the *The English in the West Indies*, gives an account of his trip on shore in the 'Don's' boat, and I can't do any better than advise people to read it.

The ship, after leaving Jacmel, coasts along the island till three o'clock in the afternoon, and gives opportunity to people to exercise themselves carrying their binoculars about; there is nothing to be seen except rugged cliffs, without anything growing on them but bush.

A few quaint people as passengers are taken on board at Jacmel, principally small traders going to Jamaica with empty trunks. At Jamaica they buy goods and return to Jacmel by the next steamer, which leaves Jamaica at 2 P.M. on the following Tuesday; they land on the Friday morning.

I have known people go from Jacmel to Jamaica to have their teeth attended to, there being no dentist any nearer.

If the morning is fine and the mountain tops are clear, the approach to Port Royal is well worth being on deck to see. In fact, excepting the entrance to the harbour of Rio de Janeiro, I know of no finer view.

People who are going to Jamaica for health should not remain longer in the lower part of the city of Kingston than necessary, as they are apt to judge of Jamaica by it and get prejudiced.

There is plenty of time for them to get their baggage passed through the Customs (this is done on the Royal Mail Wharf) and get away to Mandeville by the mid-day train. A telegram should be sent to Merritt's Hotel there, to announce their intention of putting up at it.

There is nothing to see in Kingston.

After leaving Jamaica, now the Panama Canal Works have stopped, there are very few passengers going farther, and the ship seems like a deserted house. She leaves Jamaica on the Saturday evening and goes to Colon, arriving there on the Monday forenoon. This part of the voyage is, as a rule, pretty rough, as the ship goes with the wind and the sea abeam, and across the equatorial current. I have known passengers, who have not been in the least sea-sick all the way from England, quite knocked over on this passage.

The steamer remains at Colon till the Wednesday, and there is time for tourists to visit Panama, going by rail across on the Tuesday morning, and returning by the morning train on the Wednesday, which reaches Colon about eleven o'clock.

Once a month the steamer goes up to Savanilla, where she arrives on the Thursday afternoon, and remains till the next Tuesday, giving
time to visit Barranquilla, situated on the river
Magdalena and connected with Savanilla by a
railway.

Once a month also the steamer leaves Colon for
Port Limon, where she arrives on Thursday, about
9 A.M., and remains till 5 P.M. on the Tuesday, or
possibly till the Wednesday, if it be the coffee
season. This gives time for people to visit the
cities of Cartago and San José, 5000 feet above
the sea. It also gives them a chance of getting
their necks broken, as the railway is one of the
most neck-breaking ones in the world. It rises
the 5000 feet in 104 miles, and was not properly
ballasted, the sleepers being merely placed on the
embankment until 1893. Still the trains did get
up and down without accident, but I would not
trust myself on it even now.

After leaving Savanilla or Port Limon, the
steamer returns to Colon, and leaves there finally
for England at 5 P.M. on the Friday, calling at
Jamaica, Jacmel and Barbadoes; she reaches
Barbadoes at daylight on the Saturday morning,
and leaves again at 5 P.M., and is due at Plymouth
on the Wednesday week at 9 P.M.

For people anxious to get away from England

for the worst three months of the winter, a trip to the West Indies and back will be found a very cheap and pleasant way of gaining their end.

The best way of proceeding will be to take a return ticket from Southampton to either Savanilla or Port Limon, as the case might be, with permission to remain a fortnight at Jamaica, on either the outward or the homeward vogage ; also to remain a month at Barbadoes on the homeward voyage.

A fortnight at Jamaica would be ample time to do the island well, and during the month's break at Barbadoes, return tickets to La Guayra on one part of the month, and to St. Thomas on the other part of the month, would give opportunity of seeing the whole of the Windward and Leeward West India Islands, and Caracas in Venezuela.

The whole could be done inside £100 for each person.

One great recommendation for this trip at the winter season of the year is, that no expensive outfit is necessary ; ordinary summer clothes will be found to answer, and there are plenty of opportunities to get washing done, and most people's wardrobes will run to sixteen days, which is the longest time away from a laundry,

The Company grant tickets for sixty-seven days, costing £67, but I consider this too much of a tie, so recommend the former plan, which gives more time for much the same money.

CHAPTER X.

I HAVE given the foregoing account of the routes of the Royal Mail steamships, in hopes of inducing folks to patronise them when in search of health or recreation, as I find the world in general knows very little of the West Indies, and I think it a pity that this should be the case, with such great facilities at hand for improving their knowledge of this part of the world, and its quaint negro inhabitants—the happiest and most contented people I have come across in all my travels.

I am still sailing in the 'Don,' and hope to be able to go on for a few years longer, and at least complete my fifty years' service in the Company ; forty-nine will have been put in if I live a few days longer.

I have not met with any adventures of late worth recording, except that, on 20th March, 1891, the 'Don' was the means of saving the crew of a

German vessel in a sinking condition, by taking them off in one of our boats.

For this service I was presented by the Emperor of Germany with a handsome gold watch, as also were my second officer who went in the rescuing boat, and the surgeon who attended the men whilst on board. The captain and all his crew were in a bad state from scurvy.

It is rather extraordinary that I should have been over fifty years at sea before being called upon to render any assistance to any one; also that this single instance should have been in connection with a German vessel, the Government of which country is always ready to reward handsomely any one who gives help to their subjects in the hour of need.

Had this been an English vessel, the Board of Trade might possibly have marked the occasion by sending me a 'binocular' worth about fifteen shillings; of course, in their wisdom, concluding a British shipmaster would not possess an article of such constant use !

The great amusement to me on these voyages is to watch the passengers and take note of their eccentricities. There is a Spanish proverb that every one is '*Poco Medico y Poco Lunatico*,' and I have learnt from observation that there is a great deal of truth in the saying.

Having in my time carried people of every class, from a king and queen to a Turkey rhubarb merchant, it will be admitted that my opportunities have been special, and, with my keen sense of the ridiculous, have been made the most of.

Passengers on board a steamship appear to be very different folks from what they are when on shore, but why they should be so, I have never been able to make out. They seem to forget the world nowadays is very small, and that it is very easy to find out who they are and what are their antecedents. Hence, as the saying is, they should not put on 'frills' as soon as they embark, as it immediately sets the others to work to find out all about them.

There was an instance of this in the early part of my career. A high official in one of the colonies went to England, and on his return took out a bride exceedingly handsome, and the possessor of a wonderful head of flaxen hair, in long ringlets, the admiration of everyone. Both the gentleman and lady were very exclusive, and had very little to say to anyone.

In due course they landed, and the lady and her wonderful hair became the talk of the place; still she would have nothing to say to any but the very highest in social rank.

One afternoon, when out driving, something

went wrong with the carriage, and madam, carriage, horse and all were toppled into the trench by the side of the road, and, besides other damage, the wonderful head of hair came off and went floating down, and presently was picked up by a negro, who put it on his head (negroes always carry things on their heads) and brought it back to the lady, and the whole secret was out.

The lovely hair, the envy of so many, was proved to be false, and the news quickly spread as a matter of course, and so great was the grief of the owner that she fell sick and was invalided soon after, thereby necessitating a change of post for her husband, as madam declined to return to the same colony, more particularly as, when folks began to inquire round, it was found the lady had figured in a hairdressing establishment at Bath before she was married.

I have met on board some of the most noted travellers, and have found them generally most pleasant people, and quite curiosities in their way.

In 1856 a gentleman embarked on board the 'Thames' at Carthagena, accompanied by a retriever, one of the most sagacious animals I have ever heard of, let alone seen.

Together they had travelled on foot from Buenoventura on the Pacific, to Bogota and down to Carthagena.

The gentleman carried a change of clothes and a diminutive kind of tent. The dog carried a basket saddle on his back, to which were attached a frying-pan and saucepan; in the latter were packed two plates, knife and fork, and a salt-box.

With this slender equipment, they had travelled several thousand miles, and been out in all weathers. On board the dog never left his master for long, night or day, and defied all the Royal Mail Company's regulations, going into the cabin whenever his master went, and it would have been bad for anyone who had tried to prevent him.

The gentleman and his dog landed at Grey Town, Nicaragua, and wended their way up the country, with no other object, that I could ascertain, except to take the portraits of General Walker, who was on a filibustering expedition in Nicaragua, and his faithful coadjutor, Major-General Bob Wheat.

About the same time I had a lady travelling with her maid, collecting birds, of which she had any number alive, and large quantities of skins. This pair of oddities had been nearly all over Central America, and were returning to England, _via_ St Thomas.

I have also carried, on two occasions, a lady from York who has visited nearly the whole of the habitable parts of the earth, entirely alone, and with only the clothes she had on, and a handbag with toilet requisites.

She told me she had ridden 130 miles inland in China on donkeys to see the Great Wall, and found it truthfully illustrated in the book of Marco Polo's travels.

On the first occasion she was on her way to Para, and went up the Amazon to its source, and travelled down to Arequipa on the Pacific, thence to Valparaiso by steamer, and crossed the mountains to Buenos Ayres, and home by Royal Mail steamer to Southampton.

Since then she has ridden through Siam on an elephant, and come out to the West Indies again. She would land out of the 'Don' at Jacmel, and as there was a good deal of swell on, to get her down into the boat again it was necessary for her to slide down the coffee shoot.

My officer told me she made no difficulty about it.

The great mountaineer, Mr Whimper, also took passage out in the 'Don,' with his two guides, when he went out to ascend Mount Cotopaxi.

The two guides returned in the ship, but Mr Whimper went home by some other route. The guides said they succeeded in getting to the highest peak, but the people of the country said otherwise. One thing is certain, if Mr Whimper says he reached the top of the mountain, there is no one who can contradict him, with the two guides to swear to it.

I have my own opinion about the matter. One thing I noticed, the guides had on the same suit of clothes they left England in, and although somewhat greasy-looking, they did not appear to have suffered much from such treatment as they would most likely have experienced ascending and descending Mount Cotopaxi.

Possibly Mr Whimper left the guides at the foot; who can say?

Travellers proper, as a rule, either don't see much as they go along, or else keep what they do see to themselves, as I have never got much information out of them, and don't seem to come across any of their adventures in books, to write which is generally supposed to be the object of their travels.

The travellers who see sights are the commercial gentlemen, dignified by the name of 'drummers,' who scour these countries to obtain orders for goods of various kinds, manufactured by the firms they represent.

These good people not only see things, but give an account of what they have seen.

These accounts occasionally quite put my old friend Baron Munchausen into the shade.

For instance, I came across one gentleman who

had been up the River Magdalena in the dry goods line, and on his way up one evening, when the steamer was tied up for the night, he took a stroll up the bank with his rifle (Manchester people always seem to have rifles), and had not gone far before he came to a whole family of alligators enjoying themselves in a quiet way.

Whilst he was admiring these monsters the howl of a tiger was heard, which appeared to strike consternation into the alligator party, but, of course, was of no moment to a brave 'drummer' armed with a Winchester.

The alligators appeared to hold a consultation, and, after a bit, as the tiger was still approaching, the whole family, with one exception, took to the water. The one that remained waited patiently till the tiger put in an appearance, and even then did not make a start, which very much astonished the onlooker.

Presently, the tiger got close to the alligator, and started off eating the tail of the saurian, and continued doing so till a considerable portion of it was consumed. This was too much for the 'drummer,' and he fired at the tiger and killed him.

The ball knocked out two of the tiger's teeth in its passage, which our friend picked up, and after having told me this wondrous story, he said,— 'If you don't believe it, I will show you the tiger's skin which I have in my cabin, and here are his two teeth made into cigarette holders.'

I naturally was anxious to know the reason of this one alligator's behaviour in waiting for the tiger and allowing him quietly to eat his tail off, and was told all he (the 'drummer') knew about it, was what he learnt from the Indians, who told him alligators have very great fear of tigers, and had not one alligator remained, the tiger would probably have taken to the river and spread havoc among the whole family. The one alligator remaining prevented this, and so sacrificed himself for the benefit of the others. For this Quintus Curtius kind of conduct the tailless alligator would be entitled to be fed, and piloted about by the others for the rest of his life, it, of course, being quite understood that the tiger would be satisfied with the tail of one beast for his supper, hence supplying a perfect understanding on these matters between the tigers and alligators !

Another gentleman, who travelled in the hardware line, including Indian idols to be buried, dug up again and sold to the unwary, told me, as he was riding over the country on the upper part of the Amazon, accompanied by some Indians, he saw a snake going along with the head of another snake sticking out of its mouth.

This appearing somewhat unaccountable, he

appealed to the head Indian for information. The Indian stated this was the way in which a gentleman snake made love to a young lady snake, with a view of making her his partner. He simply swallowed her, and carried her about inside of him for a month.

At the end of that time the young lady came out, and if she did not approve of the match skeedadled as fast as she could. The gentleman having fasted for so long had not power to follow her. On the contrary, if mademoiselle snake was agreeable, she remained by his side till he was strong enough to take her to his nest, which he would do in a few days, and then possibly, as the English novels say, they would live together happily ever after.

How the Indian knew all this was not mentioned ; but, if true, Miss Snake beat Jonah ten times over, as Jonah was only accommodated by the whale for three days, whereas the young lady snake gets carried about for thirty!

Apropos of the understanding existing between alligators and tigers, the Indians say when a tiger wants to get across a river, he comes down to the bank and howls in a wrathful manner, and forthwith an alligator comes to him. Mr Tiger jumps on to the alligator's back and gets carried over, and only just gets his feet wet. Nothing is mentioned as to what fare the tiger pays, but it is thought he gives the alligator a pass, which exempts him from having his tail eaten on a future occasion.

These kinds of stories, when told, as they doubtless are in the smoking rooms of commercial hotels in England, excite the curiosity of the gentlemen whose travels have been usually in civilised countries, and the result is an increase of passengers for the steam liners.

One peculiarity in the passengers who travel in the Royal Mail Line, is the way they form themselves into cliques; the people belonging to each island keep aloof from all the others.

When I first took command of the Atlantic ships I noticed this, and drew the attention of one of the smartest of the governors of the West India islands, who happened to be on board, and suggested bringing the good folks together.

' Don't you do it,' said the gentleman ; ' if you do, you may find they may very likely combine against you; you keep them as they are. I have always taken care to keep people apart in the colonies I have governed, and if I found them getting too friendly, I set to work and got them by the ears. Hence I have always been able to carry my measures and so have pleased the minister for the colonies, although I have never been a popular governor.'

I have taken this good gentleman's advice and have not, as a rule, mixed myself up with the passengers, and certainly have never taken part in any of the amusements they get up. I have followed out the plan of being friendly with all of them, and not giving preference to any.

I recommend my brother commanders to pursue the same policy, which I believe has been a tolerably successful one.

During the forty-one years I have been in command, I must have carried thirty thousand first-class passengers, and on one occasion I had on board one hundred and ten children and nurses, and have frequently had seventy.

I am now carrying the children of the third generation. I have had charge of hundreds of young ladies going out to their parents from school, and a great many going out to be married.

During the whole period not a single accident, worth calling such, has happened to any of them, to my recollection, except in the case of one small girl, jumping up to unhook the cabin door, getting her fingers jammed. But even that a piece of rag and a little Friar's balsam soon remedied.

I hope these good folks will remember all this when I send round the hat amongst them next year, and put enough in it to build me a cottage ready to live in when it pleases the directors of the Company to dispense with my services.

I will conclude this narrative by drawing a comparison between ocean steamships as they were when I first joined one, and those of the present day, not that I lately have had anything to do with the first-class ones, as younger men than myself have commanded them in the Royal Mail Line, but still I know pretty well the ins and outs of them all.

There is no doubt in my mind that the old-fashioned paddle-wheel boat was far and away more comfortable than the ship of the present day. They were *bona fide* passenger steamers, and everything was not sacrificed to cargo carrying capacity, as in the case nowadays. But then people who travelled in them had to pay well, whereas the cheap fares of the present time must be made up by numbers, hence three and four have to be berthed in one cabin, instead of each one having a whole cabin.

People formerly were satisfied to occupy twice the time on the passage they will put up with now, and extra speed means extra coal and extra expense in every way, except in feeding them, which not only costs less for each per day, but the shortness of the passage also reduces it. The new-fashioned ship also shakes them up a good deal more, and the passage, as a rule, nearly comes to an end before they want to eat at all ; in fact, I have known ladies go all the way across and only be able to take soda water and milk as nourishment.

The greatest improvement in the comfort of the ships is the electric lighting, particularly to sea-sick folks. Formerly the cabins were lighted by oil lamps which (unless ordered otherwise by the doctor) were blown out at eleven o'clock, leaving a smell behind them enough to upset anyone. Doubtless there are many still going who recollect the discomfort of being left suddenly in darkness for the whole night. Now a light can be had all night or at any time in the night at pleasure, all danger from fire being over.

There are still a great many improvements needed, and shipbuilders would do well to learn what they are.

Not long ago I read a speech made by one of these gentlemen, and in it he stated that very little dependence should be placed in the opinions of ship captains as to shipbuilding. If ship captains don't know what is wanted in the ships, pray who is likely to know?

To my fancy, shipbuilders don't, and they would do well to find out what old skippers do know, and possibly they would not turn out the failures they do. Certainly they would not con-

struct a ship so as to give the passengers the full
benefit of the smell of the heterogeneous articles
in the hold.

Only think of paying for having a cabin in
which you are subjected to the aroma of hides,
coffee, cocoa, pimento, sugar and tropical fruit
mixed. I wish I had a shipbuilder in such a
cabin, and he with a touch of malarial fever on
him!

At times, of course, the weather is such that
everything that opens to the air, can be kept
open, but should the weather change so as to
necessitate closing up, the sufferings of sick people
are then dreadful.

There is no need for this state of things. The
hatchways should be entirely apart from the
passengers' accommodation, and special ventilation
should be provided for the cargo spaces. The
cabins, also, should be rendered independent of
ventilation, either from skylights or scuttles, so
that no inconvenience should be felt when everything has to be shut up in bad weather.

A shipbuilder ought to employ a proper ventilating engineer; he would then possibly be able
to build a passenger ship in which people need
not be half suffocated in bad weather, as they
have been in every ship with which I have been
connected.

The deck houses of modern ships add materially to the comfort of the passengers, affording as they do a refuge in wet weather, with plenty of fresh air, and under the lee of them and sheltered by the promenade deck-over, deck-chairs can generally be made use of.

The refrigerators are also, to my mind, a great improvement, doing away with the necessity of carrying live stock on deck, and giving the homeward bound folks the advantage of the English market, instead of the West India as formerly.

No doubt there are many advantages in the new-fashioned ships over the original ones, but there are also many defects that require rectifying before ocean travelling can be considered that happiness it ought always, materially speaking, to be.

THE END.

LONDON : DIGBY, LONG AND CO., PUBLISHERS,
18 Bouverie Street, Fleet Street, E.C.

SUPPLEMENTARY LIST.

DIGBY, LONG & CO.'S
NEW NOVELS, STORIES, Etc.

A NEW NOVEL, by DORA RUSSELL, Author of "Footprints in the Snow," "A Great Temptation," etc., entitled **"A Hidden Chain,"** *will be ready in April, in Three Volumes, at all the Libraries.*

A NEW NOVEL, in Three Volumes, by JEAN MIDDLEMASS, Author of "A Girl in a Thousand," "Sealed by a Kiss," etc., entitled **"The Mystery of Clement Dunraven,"** *will be ready in April, at all the Libraries.*

A NEW NOVEL, in One Volume, by ALGERNON RIDGEWAY, Author of "Westover's Ward" and "Diana Fontaine," will be ready at all Libraries and Booksellers in April.

EVA TRAVERS EVERED POOLE'S NEW NOVEL, entitled **"His Troublesome Sister,"** *is now ready, in One Volume, at all Libraries and Booksellers.*

Like a Sister. By MADELINE CRICHTON. In Three Vols., crown 8vo, cloth, 31s. 6d. (SECOND EDITION.)

The *PEOPLE* says:—" We predict for her a prosperous career. She writes good English, and works out her plot with considerable skill."
The *GLASGOW HERALD* says:—" The writer possesses the faculty of depicting character with force and consistency. The literary texture is good, and the dialogue throughout is brisk and vivacious."

IN ONE VOLUME, Price **6s.**

Dr Janet of Harley Street. By DR ARABELLA KENEALY, Author of "Molly and Her Man-o'-War." Crown 8vo, cloth, 6s. (SIXTH EDITION.)

The *DAILY CHRONICLE* says:—"It is a clever book, and well worth reading Miss Kenealy has imagined an interesting character, and realised her vividly."

NEW NOVELS AND STORIES—*Continued.*
IN ONE VOLUME, Price **6s.**

What Happened at Morwyn. By MARIA A. HOYER, Author of "Good Dame Fortune." Crown 8vo, cloth, 6s.

The *PALL MALL GAZETTE* says:—"It is refreshing to take up so bright and wholesome a story as 'What Happened at Morwyn,' and one written in a style so fresh and natural. Its heroine realises as nearly as may be Wordsworth's famous description of woman as she should be. . . . Cordially recommending it to our readers.'

Upper Bohemians. By FREDERICK G. WALPOLE, Author of "Lord Floysham," etc. Crown 8vo, cloth, 6s. (SECOND EDITION.)

The *MORNING POST* says:—"An entertaining book, by a clever man of the world. Bright sketches of men and things here and abroad. The author's pictures of Roman society are excellent."

"Zorg" A Story of British Guiana. By VERNON KIRKE. Crown 8vo, cloth, 6s.

The *PUBLIC OPINION* says:—"After starting to read 'Zorg' one will not put it down until the book is finished. The novel is a promising one. The character of Sarnia Gordon is cleverly drawn: indeed all the characters are depicted in a natural and life-like manner."

The Princess's Private Secretary. From the Italian of A. G. BARRILI, by His Honour JUDGE STEPHEN. Crown 8vo, cloth, 6s. (SECOND EDITION).

THE TIMES says:—"The character drawing is full of *finesse*, and the insight which we incidentally get into the attitude of the Vatican and the ancient Roman nobility towards the *de facto* rulers of Rome, makes the book an instructive as well as an amusing one. The translation is executed with exceptional taste."

Netta. By EDWIN ELLIOTT. Crown 8vo, cloth, 6s.

The *ACADEMY* says:—"Mr Elliott is to be welcomed . . . A quite excellent story. Style . . . so good . . . Not only is the interest permanently sustained, but passages of dramatic vividness detain the reader."

West Cliff: A Romance of Portland Isle. By EASTON KING. Crown 8vo, cloth, 6s. (SECOND EDITION.)

The *MANCHESTER EXAMINER* says:—"It is an intensely interesting and very well written book, which we can heartily recommend."

A Deformed Idol. By JAMES J. MORAN, Author of "The Dunferry Risin'," etc. Crown 8vo, cloth, 6s. (SECOND EDITION.)

The *FREEMAN'S JOURNAL* says:—"His unquestioned power as a fictional writer . . . . . .The various threads are so ingeniously interwoven and artistically presented as to secure the undivided attention of all."

Maria, Countess of Saletto. From the Italian of E. ARBIB, by SYDNEY KING. Crown 8vo, cloth, 6s.

"An animated, interesting and vivid picture of Modern Italian Society."

NEW NOVELS AND STORIES—*Continued.*

IN ONE VOLUME, Price **6s.**

Marianela. From the Spanish of B. PEREZ GALDOS. By MARY WHARTON, Translator of " Lady Perfecta," from the same Author. Crown 8vo, cloth, 6s.

The *GLASGOW HERALD* says :—" One of the ablest novelists that Spain has produced."

Deferred Pay; or, A Major's Dilemma. By Lieut.-Colonel W. H. M'CAUSLAND. Crown 8vo, cloth, 6s. (SECOND EDITION).

The *SCOTTISH LEADER* says :—" A more than usually interesting novel. There is plenty of incident and adventure, and not a little fun. The story gives a soldier's life from a soldier's point of view."

Her Angel Friend. By MARY TREGARTHEN. Crown 8vo, cloth, 6s. [*Just Out.*

England against The World: A Novel. By JOHN LITTLEJOHNS, Author of "The Flowing Tide," etc. Crown 8vo, cloth, 6s. [*Immediately.*

IN ONE VOLUME, Price **3s. 6d.**

A Son of Noah. By MARY ANDERSON. Crown 8vo, cloth, 3s. 6d. (FIFTH EDITION.)

The *GUARDIAN* says :—" To have told the love story of Shem in Biblical phraseology is a deed worthy of the highest admiration, and we cannot sufficiently congratulate the authoress on the undertaking, for she has really succeeded in making it interesting. There is an excellent description of a fight with a mashtak, and the account of the Deluge is very vivid."

The Last Cruise of the Teal. By LEIGH RAY. In handsome pictorial binding. Illustrated throughout. Crown 8vo, cloth, 3s. 6d. (SECOND EDITION.)

The *SPECTATOR* says :—" The stirring tale of sea adventure which the book contains is told well and graphically enough to be very readable."
The *NATIONAL OBSERVER* says :—" It is long since we have lighted on so good a story of adventure."

In a Forest Glade. By E. ARDEN MINTY. With Illustrations by FRED PEGRAM. Crown 8vo, cloth, 3s. 6d.

The *DAILY TELEGRAPH* says :—" Presented in a graceful and pleasing guise, cleverly written and extremely readable."

---

18 *Bouverie Street, Fleet Street, London.*

NEW NOVELS AND STORIES—*Continued.*
IN ONE VOLUME, Price **3s. 6d.**

The Fate of Fred Lavers. The Story of a Lonely Life. By ALEXANDER MORRISON, Author of "The Haunted Bungalow and other Stories." Crown 8vo, pictorial cloth, 3s. 6d.

The *SCOTSMAN* says:—"Of the many stories which of late have been founded upon the art or the powers of the hypnotist or the mesmerist, there is none more remarkable or more readable than Mr Alexander Morrison's book."

The Bridal March. From the Norwegian of Björnson, and **The Watch**; an Old Man's Story. From the Russian of Ivan Turgenieff. Translated by JOHN EVAN WILLIAMS. Crown 8vo, cloth, 3s. 6d.

The *LITERARY WORLD* says:—"'The Bridal March,' with its vivid descriptions, will be read with interest. . . . Charmingly told, the characters are skilfully drawn, and stand out in strong relief. 'The Watch' is replete with vigorous touches, and wholly original. It exhibits the writer's peculiar gift of character drawing, supplemented by effective descriptive power."

Mervyn Hall. A Story of Incident. By FRANCIS R. ROBERTS. Crown 8vo, cloth, 3s. 6d.

The *FREEMAN'S JOURNAL* says:—"The tale is so artistically worked out as to secure the undivided attention of even the most *insouciant* of readers."

The Venetian Secret; or, the Art of the Past. By CHARLES LUTYENS. Crown 8vo, cloth, 3s. 6d.

The *GUARDIAN* says:—"The novel is a pleasant one. Some hunting scenes are very breezy and real, and the central figure, that of the painter, is interesting."

Keith Kavanagh Remittance Man. An Australian Novel. By E. BALDWIN HODGE. Crown 8vo, cloth, 3s. 6d. [*Shortly.*

The Bow and the Sword. A Romance. By E. C. ADAMS, M.A. With 16 full-page drawings by MATTHEW STRETCH. Crown 8vo, pictorial cloth, 3s. 6d.

The *MORNING POST* says:—"The author reconstructs cleverly the life of one of the most cultivated nations of antiquity, and describes both wars and pageants with picturesque vigour. The illustrations are well executed."

A Daughter of Rome; A Romance. From the German of LOUISA PICHLER. By J. M. COLLES. Crown 8vo, cloth, 3s. 6d.

The *GUARDIAN* says:—"The story is well told and extremely interesting."

NEW NOVELS AND STORIES—*Continued.*
IN ONE VOLUME, Price **3s. 6d.**

Irish Rebels; a Novel. By ALEXANDER M'ARTHUR. Author of "Our Musical Tour," "Nicolo Cesi," etc. Crown 8vo, cloth, 3s. 6d.

The *LIVERPOOL COURIER* says:—"This admirably well written and startling novel. . . . The story is so realistically told that few will be able to read it without quite awesome interest being aroused."

The Hero of the Pelican; An Ocean Drama. By PERCY DE LISLE. Crown 8vo, pictorial cloth, 3s. 6d.

The *PEOPLE* says:—"There is some really good writing in this volume, and the author seems to have the makings of a second Clarke Russell."

The Girl Musician. By MIRIAM YOUNG. With full-page illustrations by MATTHEW STRETCH. Crown 8vo, cloth, 3s. 6d.

The *LIVERPOOL MERCURY* says:—"This is a very pleasing story. The book is quite delightful."

The "Jolly Roger." By HUME NISBET, Author of "Bail Up," etc. With illustrations by the Author. Crown 8vo, picture boards, 2s. (FIFTH EDITION). Or in pictorial cloth, 3s. 6d.

The *SATURDAY REVIEW* says:—"Sorcery and the sea are deftly combined. Since Captain Marryat's impressive story of Vanderdecken and the fair Amine, these elements have never been handled as in Mr Nisbet's brilliant romance of Elizabethan times. In his handling of the supernatural, the author's power is most convincingly proclaimed."

The Old House of Rayner. By GRIMLEY HILL. Crown 8vo, cloth, 3s. 6d.

The *DAILY TELEGRAPH* says:—"Eminently readable. . . . Written to entertain . . . Fulfil their object very adequately."

IN ONE VOLUME, Price **2s. 6d.** and **1s.**

Clenched Antagonisms. By LEWIS IRAM. Crown 8vo, cloth, 2s. 6d.

The *SATURDAY REVIEW* says:—"'Clenched Antagonisms' is a powerfu and ghastly narrative of the triumph of force over virtue. The book gives a striking illustration of the barbarous incongruities that still exist in the midst of an advanced civilisation."

NEW NOVELS AND STORIES—*Continued.*
IN ONE VOLUME, Price **2s. 6d.**

My Village.   By R. MENZIES FERGUSSON, M.A., Author of "Our Trip North," etc., etc.   Crown 8vo, pictorial cloth, 2s. 6d.

The *LITERARY WORLD* says:—"This is an interesting book. The scenes depicted will revive in many breasts enchanting memories of bygone years, and obscure villages far away."

Dr Weedon's Waif.   By KATE SOMERS.   Illustrated with full-page drawings by MATTHEW STRETCH. Crown 8vo, cloth, 2s. 6d.

VANITY FAIR says:—"One of the prettiest and most touching stories we have read for a long time."

For Marjory's Sake: A Story of South Australian Country Life.   By Mrs JOHN WATERHOUSE.   In handsome cloth binding, with illustrations.   Crown 8vo, cloth, 2s. 6d.

The *LITERARY WORLD* says:—"A delightful little volume, fresh and dainty, and with the pure, free air of Australian country parts blowing through it . . gracefully told . . . the writing is graceful and easy."

A Stock Exchange Romance.   By BRACEBRIDGE HEMYNG, Author of "The Stockbroker's Wife," "Called to the Bar," etc., etc.   Edited by GEORGE GREGORY.   Crown 8vo, picture cover 1s.   *[Just Out.*

MISCELLANEOUS.

The Fall of Adam; A Treatise.   Demonstrating Evil in its origin to have been the resultant of Natural Law under circumstances which were peculiar to the Edenic Period of Time.   By the Rev. STEPHEN SHEPHERD MAGUTH, LL.D.   In two vols., royal 8vo, cloth, 32s.   *[Now Ready.*

The Autobiography of an Old Passport, 1839-1889, chiefly relating how we accomplished many Driving Tours with our own English Horses over the Roads of Western Europe before the time of Railways. By the Rev. ALFRED CHARLES SMITH, M.A., Author of "Attractions of the Nile," "A Spring Tour in Portugal," "A Pilgrimage through Palestine," etc.   With numerous illustrations.   Royal 8vo, cloth extra, 21s.

The *DAILY NEWS* says:—"There is a refreshing flavour in these chatty Diaries . . . these lively and amusing reminiscences. . . . There is nothing in the tours and trips of to-day to compare with them in charm."

MISCELLANEOUS—*Continued.*

Mr P.'s Diary: Facts, Ideas, Suggestions, Reflections and Confessions. By JAMES T. HOSKINS, M.A.,F.R.S.L. Royal 8vo, cloth, 21s.

The *LANCET* says:—"Full of philosophical and psychological reflection, replete with sound deductions, illumined here and there with flashes of genuine humour, the whole based upon wide experience and a large acquaintance with men and things, the volume is one that may be taken up at almost any time with profound satisfaction."

Leading Women of the Restoration. By GRACE JOHNSTONE. With portraits. Demy 8vo, cloth, 6s.

The *LITERARY WORLD* says:—"This is a very readable book. . . . This book, indeed, contains a few valuable lives, told fully and fairly, of women who deserve to be remembered."

PUBLIC OPINION says:—"This entertaining work. . . . This is essentially a book of historic value."

Three Empresses. Josephine, Marie-Louise, Eugénie. By CAROLINE GEAREY, Author of "In Other Lands," etc. With portraits. Crown 8vo, cloth, 6s.

The *TIMES* says:—"An industrious and appreciative student. . . . Tells her stories well."

The Author's Manual. By PERCY RUSSELL. With Prefatory Remarks by Mr GLADSTONE. Crown 8vo, cloth, 5s. (SIXTH EDITION.) With portrait.

The *WESTMINSTER REVIEW* says:—". . . Mr Russell's book is a very complete manual and guide for journalist and author, and those proud words 'sixth edition' on the title-page show that it has been appreciated. And it deserves to be; it is not a merely practical work—it is literary and appreciative of literature in its best sense; . . . we have little else but praise for the volume."

Sixty Years' Experience as an Irish Landlord. Memoirs of JOHN HAMILTON, D.L. of St. Ernan's, Donegal. Edited, with Introduction, by the Rev. H. C. WHITE, late Chaplain, Paris. Crown 8vo, cloth, 6s. With Portrait.

The *TIMES* says:—"Much valuable light on the real history of Ireland, and of the Irish agrarian question in the present century, is thrown by a very interesting volume entitled 'Sixty Years' Experience as an Irish Landlord. . . .' This very instructive volume."

Nigh on Sixty Years at Sea. By ROBERT WOOLWARD ("Old Woolward"). Crown 8vo, cloth, 6s. With Portrait. *[Now Ready.*

Whose Fault? The Story of a Trial at *Nisi Prius.* By ELLIS J. DAVIS, Barrister-at-Law. In handsome pictorial binding. Crown 8vo, cloth, 3s. 6d.

The *TIMES* says:—"An ingenious attempt to convey to the lay mind an accurate and complete idea of the origin and progress and all the essential circumstances of an ordinary action at law. The idea is certainly a good one, and is executed in very entertaining fashion . . . Mr Davis's instructive little book."

MISCELLANEOUS—*Continued.*

Love, Marriage, and Happiness. By "Isidore."
Crown 8vo, elegant cloth, 2s. 6d.   [*Just Out.*

Herman, and Jack Frost's Castle. By the Hon.
Mrs W. F. Maitland. In beautiful pictorial binding.
With illustrations. Small royal 8vo, cloth, 1s. 6d.

The *MANCHESTER EXAMINER* says :—"It is admirably illustrated and
most beautifully got up; a most enjoyable and welcome work for the young."

A CENTENARY MONOGRAPH.

Charlotte Corday; or, a Hundred Years After.
By Mary Jeaffreson, Author of "Roman Cameos,"
"Through all the Varying Year," etc. Crown 8vo,
cloth, 2s. 6d.   [*Just Out.*

POETRY.

The Feast of Cotytto, and Other Poems.
By Charles T. Lusted. Author of "Studies in Life
and Literature." Fcap. 8vo, cloth, 3s. 6d. [*Just out.*

An Illusive Quest, and Other Poems. By
Hollis Freeman. Crown 8vo, cloth, 3s. 6d.

The *IRISH TIMES* says:—"Will become a favourite with those who admire
poetry of a good and thoughtful class."

King William III.: An Historical Romance.
By William Joseph Yeoman. Crown 8vo, cloth,
3s. 6d.   [*Just Out.*

Some Translations from Charles Baudelaire,
Poet and Symbolist. By H. C. With Portrait.
Fcap. 8vo, elegant parchment, 2s. 6d.

The *TIMES* says:—"Are executed with no little metrical skill and command of
poetic diction."

₊ *A complete Catalogue of Novels, Travels, Biographies,
Poems, etc., with a critical or descriptive notice of each, free
by post on application.*

London: **DIGBY, LONG & CO.,** Publishers,
18 *Bouverie Street, Fleet Street, E.C.*

Milton Keynes UK
Ingram Content Group UK Ltd.
UKHW050705300424
441987UK00008B/445

9 781535 807944